AF867736

Sawan

Illustrated COMPREHENSION

A complete book for competent and enthusiastic readers

6

INCLUDES

- Poetry Comprehensions
- Enhanced Vocabulary
- Grammar Exercises
- Creative Writing
- Multiple Choice Questions (MCQs)

MANOJ PUBLICATIONS

Publisher:
MANOJ PUBLICATIONS
761, Main Road, Burari, Delhi-110084 (INDIA)
Mobile: 09999476076, 9868112194
8178823569, 8178854810
Email: info@manojpublications.com
For online shopping visit our Website :
www.sawanonlinebookstore.com

ISBN : 978-93-91460-74-7

Illustrated Comprehension - 6

Conceived by : **Sanyam Gupta**
Written by : **Prashant Gupta**
Edited by : **Rohan Kumar**

Preface

Reading is a multifaceted process that develops only with practice. There are certain aspects of reading, such as fluency and word recognition, which can be learnt in a certain amount of time. These basics must be mastered but at the same time reading comprehension should be emphasized in the process. Students can parrot words on a page all day long, but if they don't have the necessary comprehension skills, they will not be able to make predictions, monitor their understanding of content, sequence or characters, clarify the confusing text, or connect what they're reading to their own experience or prior knowledge. And that is what true comprehension is all about.

The **Illustrated Comprehension** series designed for readers of grades 1 to 6 offers reading passages with questions on a variety of topics. The main objective is to lay the foundation to build up students' confidence in tackling comprehension, to encourage higher-level thinking and understanding, and also motivate to think beyond the ideas presented in the passages or poems. It will also help them enhance their **Word Power and Grammar Skills**.

We hope the present series will prove a boon for all the students and come up to their expectations.

Suggestions for the betterment of the series are welcomed.

– Publishers

Contents

1 Friends and Flatterers

Everyone that **flatters thee**,
Is no friend in **misery.**
Words are **easy**, **like the wind**,
Faithful friends are hard to find.

Every man will be thy friend,
Whilst **thou** hast **wherewith** to spend;
But if **store of crowns** be scant,
No man will supply **thy** want.

If that one be **prodigal**,
Bountiful they will him call,
And with suchlike flattering,
'Pity but he were a king'.

But if Fortune once do **frown**,
Then farewell his great **renown**,
They that fawn'd on him before,
Use his company no more.

He that is thy friend in deed,
He will help thee in thy need,
If thou sorrow, he will weep,
If thou wake, he cannot sleep.

Thus of every grief in heart,
He with thee doth bear a part.
These are certain signs to know,
Faithful friend from flattering **foe**.

—William Shakespeare

Know These Words

flatters	–	praises someone insincerely
thee	–	you
misery	–	unhappiness/bad times
easy, like the wind	–	can move anywhere without any direction
thou	–	you
wherewith	–	money
store of crowns	–	plentiful of money
thy	–	your
prodigal	–	spendthrift
bountiful	–	plentiful
frown	–	a facial expression indicating disapproval
renown	–	fame
foe	–	enemy

Questions-Answers

A. Underline the correct answer.

1. What does the line 'words are easy' indicate?

   Tick (✓) all the correct options.

   a. taking oath of friendship is easy ☐

   b. saying flattering words is easy ☐

   c. making strong promises of keeping friendship is quite easy. ☐

   d. making fun of friends is easy. ☐

2. Meaning of word 'prodigal' in this poem–

   a. spendthrift   b. generous   c. liberal

3. ________ friends are hard to find.

   a. Stylish   b. Faithful   c. False

B. Answer the following questions.

1. Are the flattering friends true friends? If not, why?

2. What kind of friends are hard to find ?

3. What happens when our wallet is full?

4. What will a true friend do when we are in grief ?

5. What is the surest test to know a true friend ?

6. Which word has the same meaning as that of 'enemy'?

7. Find two adjectives from the poem.

Creative Writing

C. Did a friend ever point out some flaws of yours? How did you react?

D. Are you a true friend? Do you tell your friends about their flaws to help them be perfect persons?

Word Power

E. Find the given words (in the Word Bank) in the word grid.

Word Bank

anti-bullying	buddy	caring	compassionate	fresh
mean	help	friends	kindness	nice
protect	hurtful	share		

u	s	x	g	p	y	p	j	s	d	i	w	d	y	l
c	b	u	d	d	y	l	f	r	i	e	n	d	s	h
x	t	w	k	r	l	e	t	r	u	e	n	i	c	e
l	u	c	a	r	i	n	g	n	g	i	a	o	j	w
i	x	h	e	o	v	f	o	x	m	e	a	n	p	q
z	f	r	e	s	h	s	r	n	o	g	f	m	g	u
c	p	b	w	b	n	n	i	p	r	o	t	e	c	t
s	h	a	r	e	t	u	s	k	e	t	u	c	b	z
v	g	x	a	n	t	i	b	u	l	l	y	i	n	g
h	e	l	p	d	p	r	o	t	e	c	t	v	h	j
i	i	l	e	p	n	p	i	a	n	w	x	s	j	k
h	u	r	t	f	u	l	k	i	n	d	n	e	s	s
a	b	t	u	t	u	k	l	y	u	e	i	k	y	z
c	c	x	e	i	p	v	c	l	p	r	y	f	p	n
c	o	m	p	a	s	s	i	o	n	a	t	e	u	j

Grammar Skills

Components of Language

Language : System of sounds, words, patterns of verbs, etc. to communicate.

Grammar : Study of rules for forming words and combining them into meaningful sentences.

Alphabet : A set of 26 letters used in a fixed order while writing a language.

Letters : A letter is the smallest unit of language. There are two types of letters—Capital letters and Small letters

Furthermore, these letters are divided into:

a. Vowels : a, e, i, o, u

b. Consonants : b, c, d, f, g, h, j, k, l, m, n, p, q, r, s, t, v, w, x, y, z

Word : A combination of letters used in a fixed order for expressing a clear meaning.

Sentence : A group of words arranged in a particular order to make complete sense. A sentence may have two components–
Phrase and Clause

Paragraph : A distinct section of written text usually consisting of several sentences dealing with a single theme.

Prefix : A form added to the beginning of the word to modify its meaning.

Suffix : A form added to the end of the word to modify its meaning.

F. Use prefixes (un-, dis-, mis-) to find the opposites of these verbs:

1. wrap – ____________________
2. used – ____________________
3. agree – ____________________
4. fold – ____________________
5. close – ____________________
6. understand – ____________________
7. behave – ____________________
8. connect – ____________________
9. tidy – ____________________
10. honest – ____________________

G. Use suffixes (-ness, -ly, -ship, -hood, -dom) to make new words.

1. happy – ____________________
2. sad – ____________________
3. free – ____________________
4. friend – ____________________
5. neighbour – ____________________
6. weak – ____________________
7. kind – ____________________
8. bore – ____________________
9. court – ____________________
10. child – ____________________

Let Us Know More

Friends are important and can bring so much joy in our life. Let us see what our friends can do for us.

1. **Friends can raise us up or bring us down**–A great true friend will always raise you up.
2. **Friends accept our imperfections**– True friends show their true colours and the most beautiful thing is that they love each other despite their imperfections.
3. **Friendship is not about competition**– True friends are always generous and they learn to work with each other's strong points. A true friend will be clapping when you enjoy the limelight.
4. **True friends stand up for each other**– Our real friends will never feel it okay for others to speak badly about us behind our back.
5. **Friends are allowed to make mistakes**–Friends are human beings and as such, they can make mistakes sometime. They don't feel hesitation while saying sorry.

Fun Chat

Read and laugh.

Two kids brought their pets to school for show and tell.

Johnny had a mouse and Danny had a cat.

When it was Johnny's turn, he told the teacher that he didn't have anything to show.

"Why not?" the teacher asked.

"Because Danny's homework ate my homework!"

☺ ☺ ☺

2 The Mysterious Passenger

One fine morning, a young man woke up in very good mood. He was in a jolly mood as he had a sound sleep. He was a bus driver by **profession**. After getting ready, he went to the garage where his bus was parked. He took his bus out of the garage to start his morning trip. Basically, the man was of cheerful nature. Moreover, he had enjoyed a nice sleep. So, he started **plying** his bus along the scheduled route with great **enthusiasm**.

On the way to its destination, the bus was halting at all the bus-stops so that the waiting passengers might get in and those wanting to **alight** could do so. The conductor of the bus was collecting fares from the passengers. The trip was going well, until a man, who was 6 feet, 8 inches tall, boarded the bus. He was well-built, like a wrestler and he was seeming very strong. Looking at his **gigantic** figure, the bus conductor hesitated in asking him the fare. Realising the conductor's mental state, the man introduced himself, "I'm Big John and Big John doesn't pay." Both the driver and the conductor were shocked to hear his reply. At once, the morning cheerfulness of the driver faded away. Looking at Big John's physique, none of them could ask him the reason for not paying the fare. They got annoyed but could not express their annoyance as both of them were hardly five feet high and had meek thin **stature**.

The next day, the same thing happened again. The same Big John boarded the bus and gave the same reply to the conductor which **evoked** the annoyance of both the bus driver and the conductor. But, they couldn't react out of fear. The same incident continued day after day, resulting in the same reaction from both the bus driver and the conductor.

One day, the bus driver got fed up and wanted to put an end to this **whimsical** practice of Big John.

As he was physically weaker than Big John, he could not dare to face him. Instead, he signed up for a body-building programme and started learning judo, karate and other martial arts. He became quite strong by the end of summer and gathered confidence to face Big John. One fine Monday morning, Big John boarded the bus and again replied in the same tone to the conductor. The driver was already ready for the questioning. He looked straight at Big John and asked in a high voice, "But why, why won't you pay? What is preventing you from paying?" To his utter **astonishment**, Big John replied to him in a cool voice, "Big John has a bus pass!" The dumbfounded bus driver sat on his seat with utter silence.

Know These Words

profession	-	a job that needs training
plying	-	(of a vehicle) travelling regularly over a route for commercial purposes
enthusiasm	-	a strong feeling of excitement
alight	-	to get down
gigantic	-	extremely big
stature	-	natural height in an upright position
evoked	-	brought to mind
whimsical	-	strange
astonishment	-	very great surprise

Questions-Answers

A. Underline the correct answer.

1. What was the nature of the bus driver?

a. Cheerful   b. Jolly   c. Introvert

2. Who was collecting the bus fare?

a. Driver b. Conductor c. Big John

3. What was the height of Big John?

a. Five feet b. 6 feet 12 inches c. 6 feet 8 inches

4. Who learnt martial arts?

a. Big John b. Driver c. Conductor

5. What did Big John have with him?

a. Bus pass b. Bus licence c. Bus ticket

B. Answer the following questions.

1. Why was the bus driver in a good mood?

____

____

2. Why did the bus conductor hesitate in asking Big John the fare?

____

____

3. Why could the bus driver and the conductor not express their annoyance?

____

____

4. How did the bus driver feel and what did he want to do?

____

____

5. What did the bus driver learn in the body-building programme?

____

____

6. What did Big John reply to the driver about not paying the fare?

____

____

7. Do you find the story humorous? Were the driver and the conductor right to behave like that?

____

____

Creative Writing

C. Do you go to school or your relatives' home by bus? Do you buy a ticket?

____

____

D. Are you afraid of questioning stronger people? Do you think we should be brave enough to ask questions for right action?

____

____

Word Power

E. Find the words (given in the Word Bank) in the word grid.

Word Bank

aircraft	auto	biplane	boat	cart	chopper	compact
car	crane	handcar	helicopter	houseboat	limo	lorry
minivan	riverboat	rocket	tricycle	tugboat	yacht	zeppelin

l	o	r	r	y	h	h	h	a	r	a	c	y
b	e	e	y	e	e	a	a	u	o	c	o	r
i	e	t	a	e	l	n	t	t	c	r	m	a
p	p	h	c	a	i	d	r	o	k	r	p	i
l	t	o	h	i	c	c	i	m	e	i	a	z
a	u	u	t	r	o	a	c	i	t	v	c	e
n	g	s	c	c	p	r	y	n	n	e	t	p
e	b	e	h	r	t	r	c	i	c	r	c	p
b	o	b	o	a	e	r	l	v	r	b	a	e
o	a	o	p	f	r	c	e	a	a	o	r	l
a	t	a	p	t	p	a	a	n	n	a	r	i
t	e	t	e	g	c	r	e	a	e	t	r	n
a	e	e	r	a	c	t	a	l	l	i	m	o

Grammar Skills

Sentence and Its Kinds

A group of words that makes complete sense is called a sentence. There are four kinds of sentences:

Assertive Sentence : A sentence that makes a statement is called an assertive sentence.

Imperative Sentence : A sentence that expresses an order, a request or advice is called an imperative sentence.

Interrogative Sentence : A sentence that asks a question is called an interrogative sentence.

Exclamatory Sentence : A sentence that expresses a strong feeling is called an exclamatory sentence.

For example :
1. William goes to school every day. (Assertive)
2. Please help me carry this box. (Imperative)
3. How is your health? (Interrogative)
4. What an idea! (Exclamatory)

F. Read each sentence and insert the correct punctuation mark. Then, label it: imperative, assertive, interrogative or exclamatory.

1. This is our classroom — ____________________
2. How was your first day at school — ____________________
3. What a shot — ____________________
4. Get out from here — ____________________
5. Can you cancel the concert — ____________________
6. Who is the most popular singer — ____________________
7. How hot the day is — ____________________
8. Please help me carry this box — ____________________
9. Didn't you learn the tables — ____________________
10. A teacher is respected by everyone — ____________________

Let Us Know More

Human beings are simply amazing creatures. Every action and every little doing tells us how unique we are. There are things about humans and their behaviour that still manage to amaze the most famous of psychologists and stun them. There's such a mystery about us-about the different organs, about the way we think, the way we behave, etc. The most surprising human organ is the brain. It is so amazingly complex and so deep that no human has understood its true power to date. It is said that the average human uses only 10 per cent of his/her brain capacity in his/her lifetime. Imagine what will happen if the complete power is used!

Fun Chat

Brainy Riddles

Cudgel your brains and answer the riddles.

1. In a single-storey house, there are a blue sofa, blue bed, blue computer desk, blue curtains, blue carpet—everything around is blue in colour. What is the colour of the staircase?
2. What needs to be broken before you use it?
3. Why can't a man living in New York be buried in Chicago?
4. Johnny throws the ball as he could, and it comes back to him, without anybody or anything touching it. How?

3 How to Improve Your Memory

One ought to **possess** good memory to be successful in life. A person with poor memory lags behind in the rat race of competition. We must sharpen our memory skills to pass all the exams of the life with flying colours. Here are some suggestions that can enable one to sharpen one's memory skills within a short **span** of time. Meditation is one of the best methods among them.

To start with meditation, sit in a **secluded** place and close your eyes. Try to concentrate in the midst of your eyebrows on the forehead, brushing aside your thoughts. Practise meditation for at least fifteen minutes every day and you would see remarkable results of good memory power within the next 15 days.

Relaxation exercise is another method through which you can improve your memory skills. Sit or lie down on a comfortable place. Concentrate one by one on every part of the body starting from the toe. First concentrate on the left side of your body including toes, fingers, legs and eyes. Thereafter, concentrate on the right side of your body in the same manner. It will relax your body and help you sharpen your memory.

Eat nutritious diet that includes green vegetables, sprouted beans, salads and fruits for good memory. Some dried fruits, like almonds, are also very good for memory. You can take them with hot milk. Revision of lessons can also **enhance** your memory. You must try to understand your lessons first. Note down all the important points. Then revise them for at least five times to attempt your exam efficiently. Now, try one another exercise for at least 15 minutes every day. Look carefully at the things around you and then close your eyes. Now, try to recollect as many things as you can. This method can not only improve your memory but also enhance your concentration.

Last but not least, brush off all the negative thoughts. Don't say, "I can't do it." We can do everything with hard work and determination. So, always say, "I can." These suggestions will bring **rapid** improvement in your memory skills if practised regularly within a short period of time and make you one of the best students with the best memory skills.

Know These Words

possess	-	to have something
span	-	the amount of period
secluded	-	undisturbed
enhance	-	to increase
rapid	-	fast

Questions-Answers

A. Fill in the blanks.

1. Try to ____________ in the midst of your eyes on the forehead, brushing aside your thoughts.
2. We must sharpen our memory skills to be able to pass all the ____________ with flying colours.
3. Don't say, "____________ it."
4. Sit or lie down on a ______________ place.

B. Answer the following questions.

1. What is the best method to sharpen our memory within a short span of time?

   ____

   ____

2. How would you see remarkable results in your memory power within the next 15 days?

3. What should we eat for good memory?

4. What is the role of revision? How can we attempt our exam efficiently?

5. Which method enhances our memory as well as our concentration?

6. Why must we sharpen our memory skills?

Creative Writing

C. What method will you follow to improve your memory?

D. Do you forget the things fast? Do you want to sharpen your memory?

Word Power

E. Complete the crossword puzzle using the clues.

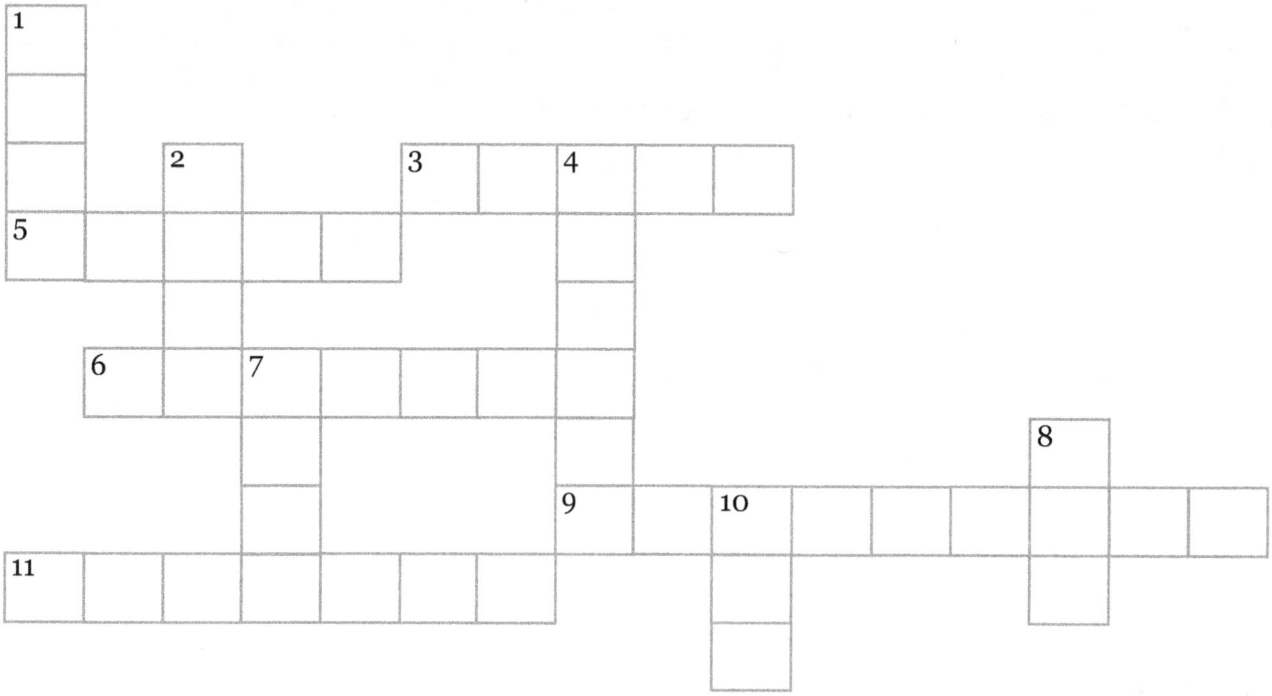

Across

3. The organ that pumps blood
5. To make letters and words with a pen or pencil
6. To accept as true, genuine or real
9. Evidence given by a witness in the court
11. Something that continues forever

Down

1. To understand something
2. The period from birth to death
4. To receive something willingly

7. Someone who doesn't speak the truth
8. The creator and ruler of the universe
10. A male child

Word Bank					
accept	believe	eternal	write	testimony	heart
life	know	god	liar	son	

Grammar Skills

Material Nouns and Concrete Nouns

A **material noun** denotes the matter or substance of which things are made.

For example : This chain is made of **gold.**

The sack is made of **jute**.

A concrete noun is the name given to a concrete thing which can be felt through our sense organs. So, all common, proper, material or collective nouns are concrete nouns.

For example : Rowdy is Sena's **brother**. (Common noun)

London is the capital of **England**. (Proper nouns)

A big **crowd** of people gathered there. (Collective noun)

My ring is made of **gold**. (Material noun)

F. Fill in the blank with the suitable material nouns using the words given in the Word Bank.

Word Bank				
iron	wood	plastic	flour	cotton

1. Try to avoid bags made of ____________.
2. I have one rod made of ____________.
3. The furniture, made of ____________, is very beautiful.
4. She was wearing a sari made of ____________.
5. Bread is made of ____________.

G. Fill in the blanks with the concrete nouns.

1. Yellow ____________ in the red vase are looking very attractive.
2. Suddenly, a black ___________ appeared when we were in the zoo.
3. My mom knows well how to make delicious ____________.
4. My ____________ is very big in which the members of my whole family can sit.
5. I always eat a hard-boiled ____________ in my breakfast.

Let Us Know More

Good memory is truly important to anyone to possess. Your memory of faces, names, facts, information, dates, events, circumstances and other things concerning your everyday life is the measure of your ability to prevail in today's fast-paced, information-dependent society. With good memory, you don't have to fear forgetting/misplacing important stuffs and you can overcome mental barriers that hinder you from achieving success in your career.

Fun Chat

Read the joke and laugh aloud.

Four monks agreed to meditate in silence for a week and not to speak a single word.

On the first day, they all maintained silence. But as darkness fell, the flame of their single candle began to flicker. "Oh, the flame is going out," said one monk.

"We should not speak a single word," said the second monk.

"Why did you two speak?"asked the third monk.

"Ha! I am the only one who did not talk!" said the fourth monk.

☺ ☺ ☺

4 Letter from a Parent

Dear Sir,
I feel I ought to write
About Tom's essay-work last night.
Of all the subjects you have set
This seemed the most unwise yet.
"Describe your family" Tom wrote it.
So well, I just had to stop it
being **handed in**; - so did my wife.
The details of our family life
Are not such a kind, alas!
That I should want them read in the class;
We did not wish the High School staff
To read them for a-lunch-hour-laugh.
We tore it out. I realise
You may think what we did unwise.
But give it your **consideration**
And please accept my **explanation**.
I trust you will not **blame** my son,
For , after all , the work was done.
Yours truly...

-Harold Honeybun

Know These Words

handed in	-	to give something to a person in authority
consideration	-	something that needs to be thought over carefully before acting.
explanation	-	the reasons that someone gives to make something clear
blame	-	to hold responsible for something bad

Questions-Answers

A. On the basis of your reading, complete the following sentences.

1. The father forbids his son to submit the essay to his teacher because

____

____

____

2. Submitting the essay to the teacher would cause the staff of the school to

____

____

____

3. According to the poet, the person to be blamed for not submitting his essay

____

____

____

4. Tom, according to his father, should be pardoned because

____

____

____

5. The letter is written to the ____

____

6. Pick out a phrase from the poem that tells us that the parent pleads with the teacher to excuse his son.

____

____

____

7. Given below is a flow chart that describes the series of events as they occur in the poem. Taking help from the bubbles given below complete the flowchart.

Tom is asked to write an essay.
a.
b.
c.
d.
The parent apologises to the teacher.

Tom writes the essay

The essay contains too many family life details

The parent tear the essay.

The parent feels it unfit to be read in the class.

Creative Writing

B. Suppose your teacher has told you to write an essay about your family. Would you write all the family details, like Tom or you will write it using your imagination?

____

____

____

____

____

____

C. **What do you think the teacher should pardon the boy for not submitting the essay? If yes, why?**

____

____

____

____

____

____

Word Power

D. **Fill in the blanks with the correct homonyms.**

1. I can _______ music. [hear/here]
2. _________, you may not enter. [Neigh, Nay]
3. The flower will (a)__________ due to scorching heat.
   The (b)_________ is green.[dye, die]
4. The (a)__________ is a small mammal.
   Her (b)____________ is thick. [hare, hair]

E. **Match the following words to their meanings.**

Column A	*Column B*
1. Hear	a. no
2. Here	b. colour
3. Nay	c. a fast-running animal with long ears
4. Neigh	d. to stop living
5. Hare	e. to receive sound through the ears
6. Hair	f. a horse's cry
7. Die	g. what grows on our heads
8. Dye	h. at in this place

Grammar Skills

Formation of Abstract Nouns

Abstract nouns can also be made from other words, such as adjectives, common nouns and verbs.

For example :

Word	–	*abstract noun*
sad	–	sadness
act	–	action
brave	–	bravery
friend	–	friendship
see	–	sight

F. Change the following words into abstract nouns.

1. wise	________________	2. proud	________________
3. kind	________________	4. know	________________
5. courageous	________________	6. intelligent	________________
7. locate	________________	8. agree	________________
9. attach	________________	10. child	________________
11. attract	________________	12. argue	________________

Let Us Know More

It is **very important to take care of the people who raise us so lovingly and affectionately. Let us know the important points that inspire us to respect our parents.**

1. **They're older and wiser–** They have spent a few more years than us which means that they have seen the world more than us and have gathered a vast experience, which shouldn't be underestimated.

2. **They're there for you, no matter what you are–** They have been with you for the last many years and have provided conducive atmosphere for your growth.

3. **They're usually right–** We have to admit that on 99% occasions, the parents speak the truth. Whatever they have done is for your betterment.

4. **They know you better than you–** They have been understanding your needs and fulfilling all your requirements without you asking.

5. **They're proud of all your achievements–** They are probably the ones who are really happy and proud of all the achievements you get in your life.

Fun Chat

Read the joke and laugh aloud.

Teacher : Did your father help you with your homework?
Student : No. He did it all by himself.

☺ ☺ ☺

Teacher : Which is more important to us, the sun or the moon?
Pupil : The moon!
Teacher : Why?
Pupil : The moon gives us light at night when we need it but the sun gives us light only in the daytime when we don't need it.

☺ ☺ ☺

5 Pride Hath A Fall

Once, there was a very tall, strong and **stout** mango tree. It was very proud of its stature and used to **mock** at other trees and plants, especially those who were lean and thinly built. One of that type of plants was a paddy plant which used to swing in happiness every day while the wind blew. He was so happy that he never felt sorrow for his thinly structure. But, the mango tree often went after the paddy plant as if the latter had not been happy with his small and weak physique.

The mango tree said to the paddy plant, "Hey paddy plant, I am sorry to see that you are so lean, thin and weak. Look at me. I am tall, strong and stout. I always stand straight as if I would **pierce** the sky and the clouds." The paddy plant answered, "Dear mango tree, I know that I am thin and short. But, I am content with my stature and never feel sorry for it. On the contrary, I thank God for sending me in this beautiful world. I always express my **indebtedness** to God for it." The mango tree heard it and gave a smile of mock at the paddy plant. After this incident, both of them were spending their days in their own way. Nobody was interfering in each other's personal life. But, the mango tree was not happy with the physical status of the paddy plant and the disadvantages it was bearing, according to him.

One day, the mango tree noticed a bee on the head of the paddy plant. It made the paddy plant lean forward. The mango tree could not tolerate it. He instantly reacted, " You are a

cursed child of Mother Goddess. She has not given you that much of strength to bear the load of even a small bee. Why aren't you cursing her? If I had been in your place, I would have surely cursed Mother Goddess for my weak physique." The paddy plant gave a smile without expressing any word. But, being mute, he told himself, 'O mango tree, you are very proud of your physique. But, you do not know that pride results a person to fall downward. You are probably moving that way.'

Days passed by. Suddenly, one day a fierce storm blew. Many houses and electric pillars were uprooted. Many people died. The proud, strong and stout mango tree was also not spared. The fierce storm uprooted the proud mango tree and made it fell with a deep and heavy thud. But, the paddy plant managed to save its life. His **frail** and **fragile** physique saved him. The mango tree paid the price with his life for his pride.

Therefore, remember that all of us are directed by God. He blesses us by bestowing good health, comfort and success, but we should not be proud of it. We should thank God for all of His blessings. The moment we become proud of our fortune, He teaches us a lesson in some way or the other.

Know These Words

stout	-	physically strong
mock	-	to make fun of someone
pierce	-	to pass through with a sharp-pointed object
indebtedness	-	the feeling of gratitude for a favour
cursed	-	damned
frail	-	weak and delicate
fragile	-	easily damaged

Questions-Answers

A. Underline the correct answer.

1. What was thinly and weakly structured?

   a. Mango tree   b. Paddy plant   c. both a and b

2. The Paddy plant was ___________ his stature.

a. content with
b. proud of
c. thankful for

3. According to the _______, the __________ was a cursed child of Mother Goddess.

a. mango tree, paddy plant
b. paddy plant, mango tree
c. neem tree, paddy plant

4. Who mananged to save its life?

a. Neem tree
b. Mango tree
c. Paddy plant

5. Who should we be thankful to?

a. God
b. People
c. Plants

B. Answer the following questions.

1. Write the structure and nature of the mango tree?

____

____

2. What was the nature of the paddy plant?

____

____

3. Why did the mango tree call the paddy plant a cursed child?

____

____

4. How was the proud mango tree uprooted and what happened to him?

____

____

5. How did the paddy plant manage to save his life?

____

____

6. Why did the paddy plant thank God?

____

____

7. Why should we thank God every day?

____

____

Creative Writing

C. Do you think people should be proud of good health, good wealth and success provided by God?

Word Power

D. Complete the following crossword puzzle using the clues.

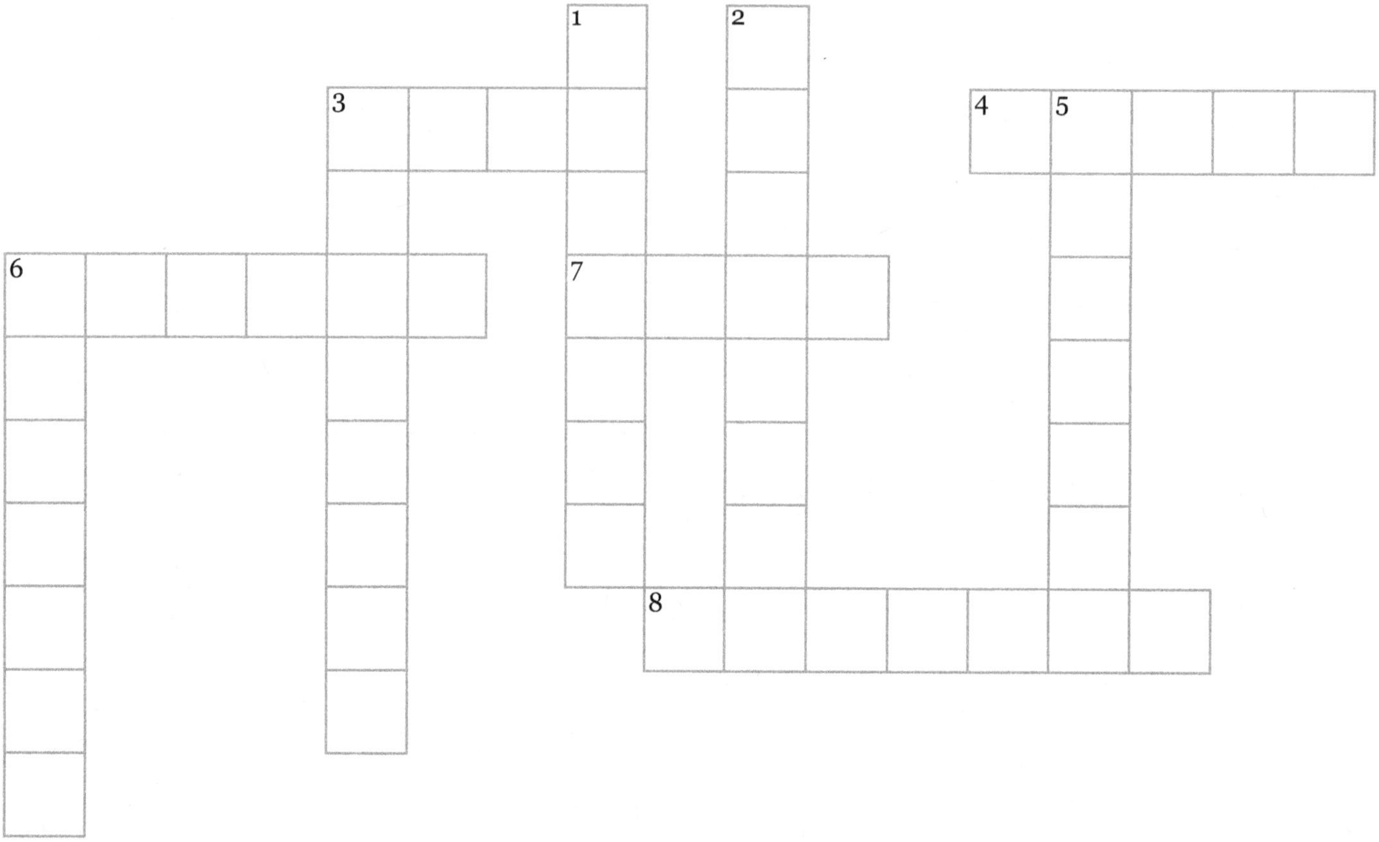

Word Bank					
soul	rejoice	blessed	hungry	servant	glorify
humble	proud	rich	merciful		

Across

3. The spiritual part of humans which lives forever
4. To be filled with excessive self-esteem
6. To feel the need or desire for food
7. Having great wealth
8. Good things given to you, especially from God

Down

1. To give honour, praise and adoration to others
2. To show mercy or compassion to others
3. One who yields or surrenders to the will or authority of another
5. To express great joy or happiness
6. Not proud or boastful

Grammar Skills

Pronouns

The words that we use in place of nouns are called **pronouns**.

Personal Pronouns

The pronouns that stand for persons, animals or things are called **personal pronouns**.

First person – The person who speaks (as I, me, us, ours, mine)

Second person – The person spoken to (as you, yours)

Third person – The person spoken about (as he, him, she, it, they, her, etc.)

For example : She gave me a gift.

Possessive pronouns

The pronouns which indicate possession are called **possessive** pronouns.

Mine, ours, yours, his, hers, theirs are possessive pronouns.

For example : That purse is mine.

E. Choose the correct personal pronoun to replace the highlighted word/words. Then rewrite the sentence.

1. The bus stopped for **William**.

____

2. **Olivia** and **Emma** bought a dress.

____

3. They fought against **Sophia** and **James**.

____

4. The teacher loved **the children**.

____

5. Count **the pens**.

____

6. The boys are tall. **The boys** can reach the top of the shelf.

____

F. Transform each sentence using a possessive pronoun.

Example:

1. This is my bag. — This bag is mine.
2. This is his room. — ____________________
3. That is their house. — ____________________
4. These are their books. — ____________________
5. Those were our balls. — ____________________
6. This was her pen. — ____________________
7. Those are your trees. — ____________________
8. This is our kitchen. — ____________________

Let Us Know More

There are two kinds of pride–good and bad. Pride may have more effects on our life and attitudes than we realise. Good pride is seeking knowledge with a pure heart that has love for God, others and self. There is nothing wrong with being confident and having pride in what we accomplish as long as we have the right attitude towards humanity. We may think that we are better than others. We have self-centred nature from birth that wants to promote an arrogant pride. This bad and arrogant pride can cause envy, jealousy, greed, hate, etc. This pride has the tendency to attract the attention of others around us. We should try to protect ourselves from this kind of pride.

Fun Chat

Read the joke and laugh aloud.

Read the joke and laugh aloud.

Why did grandpa put wheels on his rocking chair?
Because he wanted to rock n' roll!

☺ ☺ ☺

How do you know that carrots are good for the eyes?
You never see a rabbit wearing glasses!

6 Importance of Prayer

Prayer to the Omnipotent God is the most important part of our life. The people of the modern world have forgotten God and are wasting their time and money on useless and meaningless **pursuits**.

The life without a sincere prayer to God is meaningless. God is the generator, organiser and destroyer of mankind.

God is the Supreme Power of Energy. He has created everything with the **expansion** of his energy. He is Formless yet He can take any form. He is Peaceful and Celestial Light of Energy.

God has formed **numerous** plants, animals, men, **demigods**, suns, moons, stars and planets with His energy. He creates and **annihilates** His creation again and again. No one can go against His will. God is the destroyer of devils. He gives reward to the righteous and punishes sinners. So, one must make it a daily routine to pray to the Almighty God.

We should not get influenced by ignorant people who take us away from God in the name of modernity. Modernity means to become cultured, decent, sophisticated and fashionable; but, it doesn't mean to forget God. We must understand that all the beggars, the handicapped and the poorest of the poor that we see, are suffering from the punishment of forgetting Him.

The persons who forget God are the greatest sinners on the Earth. They are bound to suffer from dire consequences.

If you want to achieve success, wealth and honour in this world, then, you should never forget to pray to God from your heart, soul and mind every day.

Know These Words

pursuits	-	acts of searching for someone or something
expansion	-	the action of becoming larger
numerous	-	great in number
demigods	-	beings who are partly humans and partly God
annihilates	-	destroys

Questions-Answers

A. Underline the correct answer.

1. What is the meaning of Omnipotent?

   a. All-powerful b. Distrustful c. Respectful

2. What is life without prayer?

   a. Good b. Hell c. Meaningless

3. Who is the destroyer of devils?

   a. God b. Animal c. Mankind

4. The persons who forget God are the greatest ________ on the Earth.

   a. poor men b. cultured c. sinners

B. Answer the following questions.

1. Who do the people of the modern world have forgotten? How are they wasting their time?

   ____

   ____

2. What has God formed?

   ____

   ____

3. Why should we pray to the Almighty God daily?

4. What does modernity stand for?

5. What must we understand?

6. What kind of persons forget God?

7. If we want to achieve success then what should we do?

Creative Writing

C. Do you pray to God every day?

D. Have you ever thanked God for fulfilling your wishes?

Word Power

E. Complete the crossword puzzle using the clues.

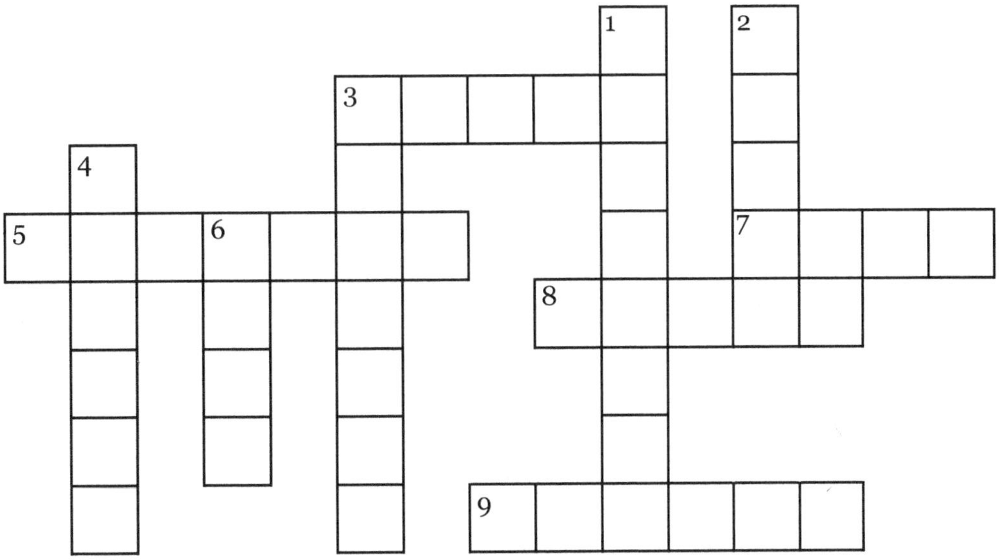

Across

3. Something you do to help someone
5. A person who speaks for God
7. Information about recent events
8. The opposite of bad
9. A long roll of paper with writing on it

Down

1. A person who is kept in jail
2. Unable to see
3. To be allowed to do whatever you want to do
4. To deliver a sermon
6. Having little or no wealth

Word Bank					
	prisoner	favour	good	prophet	poor
	blind	freedom	news	preach	scroll

Grammar Skills

Reflexive Pronouns

The pronouns that end with -self or -selves are **reflexive** pronouns.

For example :

myself, yourself, ourselves, himself, herself

A reflexive pronoun reflects back on its subject.

We can use a reflexive pronoun as an object of the verb.

For example:

He fell down and hurt **himself.**

I wash my clothes **myself.**

Emphasising Pronouns

The pronouns which are used for stressing nouns or pronouns are called **emphasising** pronouns.

For example :

myself, yourself, themselves, itself.

We put these pronouns near the subjects.

We cannot use an emphasising pronoun as an object of the verb.

For example :

I **myself** wash my clothes.

She **herself** is responsible for her sorrow.

F. Fill in the blanks with reflexive/emphasising pronouns.

1. My mother hurt __________ while cutting the vegetables with a sharp knife.
2. The players carried the injured player out of the field __________.
3. The girl __________ drove the car up the hill.
4. They should __________ go and solve the matter.
5. She ironed the clothes __________.
6. I __________ solved the problem.
7. We __________ carried the heavy bags.
8. The village __________ is not very large.

Let Us Know More

Morning is the best time to pray to God. It helps us remind that we are alive and it also connects us with the living God. He loves children and loves to listen to their prayers. Daily prayer gives us the chance to express gratitude for the things in life that God has provided us. Prayer brings us closer to God. In any relationship, communication is the key to success. Prayer is the way to communicate with God. Daily prayer protects us from the difficulties of life. It removes obstacles from our path and leads us to success.

Fun Chat

Solve these funny riddles with your friends.

1. I make a loud sound when I'm changing. When I do change, I get bigger but weigh less. What am I?
2. A bus driver was heading down a busy street in the city. He went past three stop signs without stopping, went the wrong way down a one-way street, and answered a message on his phone. But the bus driver didn't break any traffic laws. How?

7 Students and Discipline

Discipline means complete **obedience** to certain rules and regulations. It is important for the progress of society and the development of one's personality as well. It is all the more important for students.

Since a student's life is a period of learning and **grooming**, a student needs to be sincere, dedicated, firm and focused to his goals. Discipline plays a significant role in shaping one's personality and moulding one's character.

A student needs to be very punctual to his routine. He should be very regular and sincere to his studies. He should be hard-working. He should always be ready and active in various other extra-curricular activities. He should remain active and smart. He should learn how to face difficult situations and to win over them.

A student is the future of the country. It is he who has to take the responsibility of the country. He should be healthy and fit. Physical education is as important for students as to be studious and sincere at studies. A student should always be in good health and fitness. For this he should get up early in the morning. He should take exercise daily. He should play games of his

choice daily. It is well known that a healthy body has a healthy mind. His mind will be strong and sharp only when he is physically strong, fit and healthy.

The biggest task of a student is to study. A student should be very devoted and sincere to his studies. He should be very punctual. He should know the importance of time. He should regularly do his homework. He should have an **urge** to learn new things. He should have respect for his teachers and elders. He should be very cooperative with his friends. He should help the needy.

Discipline demands self-control and dedication. The one who cannot control himself cannot control others. He has to dedicate his individuality in the larger interest of the society. Discipline is a **virtue**. It needs to be cultivated from early childhood. It cannot be developed overnight. It takes time and requires patience. When discipline is enforced, it fails to bring the desired result. True **essence** of discipline is lost when it is enforced. The man becomes more a machine and less a human being.

A student's life is the formative period of life. The foundation of adulthood is laid down during that time. The man grows with the habits and manners acquired at that time. These things hardly change. So, a student should be much disciplined in this formative period. The one who is disciplined raises high in life. Life of great men is an example of discipline. The great men have made mark in their life because they strictly follow their goals with all the **earnestness** and sincerity.

So, we should try to be disciplined from the early stage of life. Both at school and at home they should be made to follow the rules of discipline. Parents, teachers and elders have a significant role to play. A student should always learn good habits. This will lead to the formation of a good society and nation as well.

Know These Words

obedience	-	doing or willing to do what you have been told to do by someone in authority
grooming	-	the things that people do to keep themselves clean
urge	-	desire
virtue	-	behaviour showing high moral standards
essence	-	the most important quality of something
earnestness	-	determination and seriousness

Questions-Answers

A. Underline the correct answer.

1. What is important for the progress of the society?
   a. Rules b. Education c. Discipline
2. Who is the future of the country?
   a. Politician b. Student c. A good parent
3. What is the biggest task of a student?
   a. To study b. To play games c. To be regular
4. What demands self-control and dedication?
   a. Education b. Discipline c. Patience
5. Whose life is an example of discipline?
   a. Great men b. Doctors c. Teachers

B. Answer the following questions.

1. What does discipline mean?

   ____

   ____

2. What is a student's life?

   ____

   ____

3. What does a student need to do to achieve his goals?

   ____

   ____

4. What should a student learn to win over difficult situations?

   ____

   ____

5. How will a student's mind be strong and sharp?

   ____

   ____

6. What happens when discipline is enforced?

____

____

7. Write any five qualities that a student must have to be disciplined.

____

____

8. Why should a student be much disciplined during his school days?

____

____

9. Find any three adjectives from the paragraph.

a. ______________ b. ______________ c. ______________

Creative Writing

C. What is the importance of discipline in our life ?

____

____

____

____

____

____

____

D. Write any five qualities you have that prove you are a disciplined student.

____

____

____

____

____

____

____

Word Power

E. Make five pairs of synonyms from the words given below:

small	timid	huge	puny	rash
cowardly	enormous	ancient	reckless	old

F. Make five pairs of antonyms from the words given below:

wild	often	proud	bright	seldom
dull	smile	frown	humble	tame

Grammar Skills

Distributive Pronouns

When the pronouns **each**, **either**, **neither** refer to persons or things one at a time, they are called **distributive** pronouns.

For example : **Either** of the boys made a mistake.
Each of his daughters studies hard.

Relative Pronouns

A relative pronoun refers to the noun or pronoun that has been mentioned earlier in a sentence. It is used for joining two sentences. **Who**, **whom**, **whose**, **which**, **that**, etc. are relative pronouns

For example :
1. This is the man. He was knocking at the door.
   This is the man **who** was knocking at the door.
2. This is the girl. I teach her English.
   This is the girl **whom** I teach English.

G. Choose the correct pronouns and complete the following sentences.

1. ____________ of them is excited about this project. (Every/Neither)
2. ____________ of the players will get the cup. (Either/Every)
3. ____________ of you can carry these boxes. (Every/Neither)
4. ____________ of you could go to receive the teacher. (Each/Either)
5. ____________ of the culprits was punished. (Every/Neither)

H. Join the following pairs of sentences by using proper relative pronouns.

1. Show me the way. The way leads to the school.

____

____

____

2. He is a man. He is never satisfied.

____

____

____

3. This is a woman. Her son has gone to the U.S.A.

____

____

____

4. The beggar was blind. We helped him.

____

____

____

5. This is a house. It belongs to my uncle.

____

____

____

Let Us Know More

In today's world, high productivity is worshipped. But how do you improve your productivity? One of the best ways to do that is to develop discipline the way you work. A disciplined mind isn't easily distracted. It knows that the work in front of it is of higher importance, and before it is completed, those distractions shouldn't be entertained.

A disciplined person has more time in a day than an undisciplined person. More time means there is more chance to do extra work or other pending work. We can overcome delay and laziness at work.

Do remember — "A disciplined mind leads to happiness and an undisciplined mind leads to suffering."

Fun Chat

Read the lines and laugh aloud.

If a barber makes a mistake
It's a new style.
If a politician makes a mistake
It's a new law.
If a scientist makes a mistake
It's a new invention.
If a tailor makes a mistake
It's a new fashion.
If a teacher makes a mistake
It's a new theory.
If a student makes a mistake
It's a mistake.

☺ ☺ ☺

8 Which Loved Best?

"I love you, Mother," said little John;
Then forgetting his work, his cap went on,
And he was off to the garden-swing,
And left her the water and wood to bring.

"I love you Mother," said rosy Nell,
"I love you better than tongue can tell."
Then she teased and **pouted** full half the day,
Till her mother **rejoiced** when she went to play.

"I love you Mother," said little Fan.
" Today I'll help you all I can,
How glad I am that school doesn't keep!"
And she rocked the babe till it fell asleep.

Then stepping softly she fetched the broom
And swept the floor and dusted the room;
Busy and happy all day was she,
Helpful and happy as child could be.

"I love you, Mother," again they said,
Three little children going to bed,
How do you think their mother guessed
Which of them really loved her best?

– Joy Allison

Know These Words

pouted	-	pushed the lips forward as a sign of annoyance
rejoiced	-	became happy

Questions-Answers

A. What do these words mean in the poem? Underline the correct option.

1. He was off to the garden-swing—
   a. He went to play on the swing in his yard
   b. He went to swing the hoes hidden in the vegetable garden
2. And left her the water and wood to bring—
   a. His mother had to bring in the wooden toys that had been left outside.
   b. His mother had to bring in wood to burn in the family's stove
3. Till her mother rejoiced when she went to play—
   a. Her mother didn't love her or want to be around her.
   b. Her mother was relieved because she was tired of hearing her remarks and seeing her frustration.
4. How glad I'm that school doesn't keep!—
   a. I am glad that there is no school today.
   b. I am glad that there is school today.

B. Answer the following questions.

1. How many children had the mother?

   ____

   ____

2. Which of them said that they loved the mother?

   ____

   ____

3. How could John have helped his mother?

   ____

   ____

4. Why was the mother happy when Nell went out to play?

____

____

5. What was it that kept Fan happy all day?

____

____

6. Which of the children do you think loved his/her mother best?

____

____

7. Write any three pairs of rhyming words from the poem.

   1. ____
   2. ____
   3. ____

Creative Writing

C. Do you love your mother ? How do you show her your love?

____

____

____

____

____

D. How do you come to know that your mother loves you a lot? Do you respect the love of your mother?

____

____

____

____

____

Word Power

F. Find the words (in the Word Bank) in the word grid.

Word Bank

attachment	devotedness	devotion	fondness
love	passion	endearment	dedicate

e	i	e	f	a	s	c	i	n	a	t	i	o	l	o	v	e
c	a	f	o	n	d	n	e	s	s	o	m	e	v	a	a	s
o	s	l	f	a	y	c	c	p	l	n	c	o	n	t	d	p
m	t	l	a	d	e	d	i	c	a	t	e	s	t	e	e	e
a	t	t	a	c	h	m	e	n	t	d	o	r	n	l	v	e
l	e	r	r	s	l	g	h	g	o	m	a	i	i	s	o	e
i	m	e	n	d	e	v	o	t	e	d	n	e	s	s	t	a
n	e	m	e	m	r	l	a	n	t	e	h	n	e	u	e	a
e	n	e	n	d	e	a	r	m	e	n	t	l	t	z	d	r
s	i	n	s	n	l	s	o	o	p	t	i	i	a	r	n	y
s	d	e	v	o	t	i	o	n	i	c	r	w	r	j	e	r
f	e	r	n	s	l	c	l	s	a	h	s	c	t	r	s	t
e	r	e	l	s	n	i	i	c	c	t	l	r	i	o	s	e
s	s	o	p	a	s	s	i	o	n	a	t	e	s	m	o	m
s	y	i	c	e	q	u	u	l	s	o	f	r	t	a	k	m

Grammar Skills

A **phrase** is a group of words that does not make complete sense. It is the part of a sentence but it does not have a finite verb.

For example : 1. The teacher threw the book **out of the window**.

2. This necklace is made **of gold**.

1. Noun phrase

A group of words that does the function of a noun in a sentence is called a **noun phrase**.

For example : 1. **Your sudden resignation** is not good for the school.

2. **A seventy-year-old woman** was sitting in the garden.

2. Adjective phrase

A group of words that does the function of an adjective in a sentence is called an **adjective phrase**.

For example : 1. My friend is a man with **good habits**.
2. An almirah is **made of steel**.

3. Adverb phrase

A group of words that does the function of an adverb in a sentence is called an **adverb phrase**.

For example : 1. Kate searched for her purse at **every place**.
2. Please arrange the medicines **in the store-room**.

4. Prepositional Phrase

The phrase which starts with a preposition is called a **prepositional phrase**.

For example : 1. Father sacrifices his life **for the sake of his children**.
2. **In case of fire**, call the fire brigade.

E. Underline the phrase and tell its kind (noun, adjective, adverb or prepositional)

1. We hope to win the first prize.
____

2. The girl in the brown frock is my sister.
____

3. She always drives with care.
____

4. The train stopped at Victoria Terminal.
____

5. They were shouting in a loud voice.
____

6. This pie is very delicious.
____

7. The candy was dark and brown.
____

Let Us Know More

14th may is celebrated as 'Mother's Day'. We sometimes forget how much our moms do for us. We must tell our moms how much we love them.

Here are five ways to show our mom how she is loved:

1. We must spend time with her. We should try to make this day about her. We must ask her what she wants to do and how she wants to spend the day doing it.
2. We should tell our mom how much we love and care for her. The right words can brighten her day.
3. We should show her how much we appreciate for her gift. It is not about the price of the gift, but the feelings of mother about us.
4. We must say "thank you" for all the helpful advice, being a great role model, time spent with us all the day. We must let her know what a great impact she has made on our life.
5. We must remember that she has showered his love on us unconditionally. Mothers day is great, but we must not wait for this day to show our love.

Fun Chat

Riddle Time

Guess the answers to the given riddles.

1. A mother has 6 girls and each of them has a brother. How many children are there?
2. If your uncle's sister is not your aunt, what is she to you?

9 An Invaluable Gift of Love

Once, there lived a sweet little girl. She was as charming as a red rose that **blossoms** early in the morning. She was four years old. One day, she took a piece of golden wrapping paper from her father's collection in order to play with it. As her father was not rich, he became **infuriated** when he saw her daughter decorating a box with that paper for the Christmas, to be given away as a Christmas gift.

He asked his daughter, "What are you doing with this paper? Don't you know how costly this paper is? I have bought this paper to use for my own purpose, and you are wasting it. Why?" The little daughter **pouted** her lips and answered, "I am not wasting this paper, dad. I am doing something special." Tears rolled down from her eyes, unnoticed by her father.

The next morning, the girl came to her father with a gift wrapped with the golden paper. The father, **embarrassed** by his earlier over-reaction, received the gift with great pleasure. When he unwrapped the box and opened it, he found nothing inside it. Again, he became very angry. He asked his daughter, "Haven't you learnt that an empty box should not be gifted to anybody? It should be filled with something worth a gift."

Again, tears rolled down her eyes and she answered, "Oh dad! The box is not empty. I have blown some kisses into this box. They all are for you." The father was again very much pained. He put his arms around his little daughter and begged her for **forgiveness**.

After a few months, the things turned bitter. The little girl met with an accident and died. The father became **unconsolable**.

Suddenly, he discovered that gift box. It is said that he kept that box by his bedside for many years and, whenever he felt discouraged, he would take out an imaginary kiss and remember the love of his little daughter who had put it in that box.

In the real sense, each one of us, as human beings, has been given a gold container filled with unconditional love and kisses from our children, the members of our family, friends and God. There is simply no other possession, which one could hold more precious than love.

Know These Words

blossoms	-	(of a tree or bush) produces flowers
infuriated	-	extremely angry
pouted	-	pushed the lower lip forward to show your annoyance
embarrassed	-	feeling ashamed
forgiveness	-	pardon
unconsolable	-	heart-broken

Questions-Answers

A. Underline the correct answer:–

1. The girl blossomed like a–
   a. red rose b. white rose
   c. jasmine flower d. cherry
2. The girl was decorating the box for a–
   a. Diwali gift b. New Year's gift
   c. Christmas gift d. Birthday gift
3. The box was filled with–
   a. chocolates b. berries
   c. toys d. kisses
4. The girl died because–
   a. she was not well b. she met with an accident
   c. she killed herself d. she was murdered

5. What message does the writer want to convey?
   a. Gifts are valuable
   b. Money should be the priority
   c. Unconditional love is the only gold
   d. None of the above

B. Answer the following questions.

1. What did the girl take from her father's collection?

   ____

2. What did he ask his daughter?

   ____

3. What was the reaction of the girl after listening to his father?

   ____

4. What did the girl give to her father next morning?

   ____

5. What was the reaction of her father after unwrapping the box?

   ____

6. How did the little girl die?

   ____

7. What did the father discover suddenly?

   ____

8. What did the father do with that box?

   ____

Creative Writing

C. When someone gives you a gift, how do you measure it—by its cost or by the feelings of the giver?

____

____

____

____

Word Power

D. Solve the following puzzle by writing the synonyms of the given words:

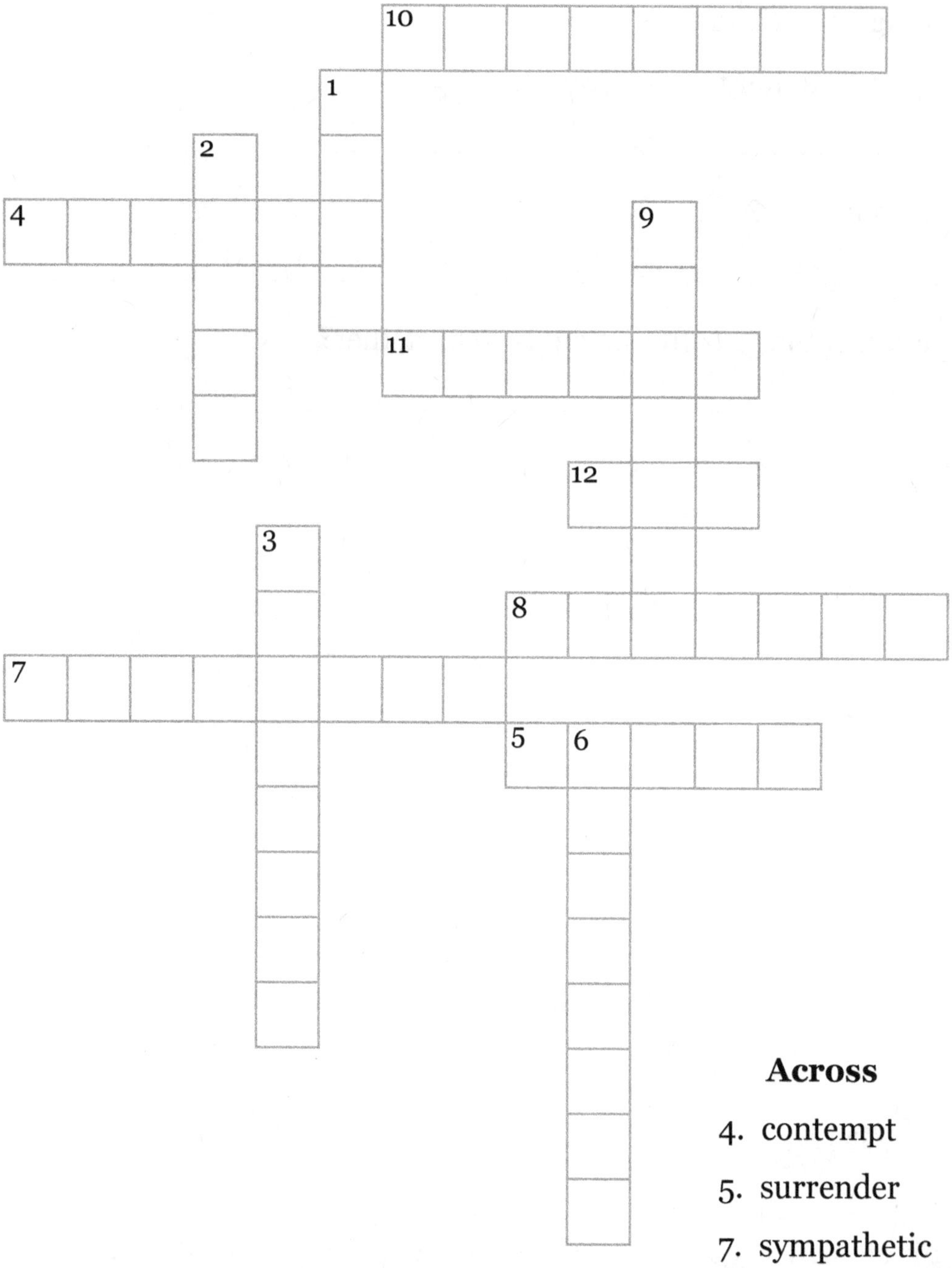

Across

4. contempt
5. surrender
7. sympathetic
8. hide
10. reduce
11. hurt
12. evil

Down

1. impolite
2. faith
3. appropriate
6. breach
9. sure

Grammar Skills

Clauses

A clause is a group of words that contains a subject and a finite verb. A clause forms part of a sentence.

For example : 1. My father gave me a **gold chain**.
2. My father gave me a chain **which was made of gold**.

In the first sentence, the word **gold chain** is a phrase. But in sentence 2, the expression **which was made of gold** has a finite verb (**made**) and has a subject (**which, used for chain**). Hence, it is a clause.

Types of clauses :

1. Main or Independent or Principal clause
2. Subordinate or Dependent clause

- A clause that has a **subject** and a **finite verb** and makes complete sense by itself is called a **main** or an **independent** or a **principal** clause.
- A dependent clause depends on the main clause to make complete sense; it is also called a **subordinate** clause.

For example :

1. James drives to work early (1) so that he may avoid being late (2).
2. James drives to work early (**James** is subject and **drives** is a finite verb). It is a clause. Also, it makes complete sense. So, it is the principal Clause.

In part 2 of the sentence, "**so that he may avoid being late**" gives an additional information about the main clause. Also, it does not make complete sense. Hence, it is a dependent clause.

E. Underline the subordinate clause in each of the sentences below.

1. Sherry enjoyed playing football, especially when her father asked her to take part.
2. When William was standing next to his sister, he looked very tall.
3. They finished the walk, which seemed never-ending.
4. Even though he had little patience, Robert enjoyed the class.
5. Sujie's skills were good although she had not been playing for long.

Let Us Know More

Children are often considered to be the most precious and valuable gifts for parents. They are loved by their parents from the core of their hearts. No matter how a child is, parents never stop caring for them. This is the purest and unconditional type of love. Parents are willing to sacrifice anything for their children. Parents are the first teachers of a child. They are not only their guardians, but also are supposed to be their best friends. All that a relationship needs is to have good understanding and ample communication. It helps children to grow properly. If a child does not have good relations or communication with his or her parents, it affects his/her future. This behaviour will reflect in his/her treatment since he/she will also treat his/her children the same way as he/she was treated.

Fun Chat

Read the joke and laugh aloud.

Teacher : "What time it be if Godzilla came to school?"

Johny : "Time to run."

☺ ☺ ☺

Paul And Henry Are Walking On A Road, And They Find A 1000 Rupee Note Lying Down.

Paul : What Should We Do Now?

Henry : We'll Take 50:50.

Paul : What About The Remaining 900?

☺ ☺ ☺

Robert : Whose Skeleton Is That?

James : An Old King's Skeleton.

Robert : Who's That Smaller Skeleton Next To It?

James : That Was Same King's Skeleton When He Was A Child.

☺ ☺ ☺

10 Etiquette and Good Manners

Good manners reveal a person's **upbringing**. They speak about not only that particular person but also his or her family. It is at home that we accquire most of our habits. Children always copy the behaviour of their parents and elders.

We should try not to hurt others by our speech or action. We should always try to be kind and polite to everyone. It is important to listen when the other person is speaking. Without good manners, much of the **charm** of life could be lost. The way you reflect your manners, others also do the same. **Courtesy** begets courtesy. Good manners also reflect good conduct and character.

They represent the social and cultural progress of the society. Good manners are the other side of culture and good education.

A cultured and educated person is always well-mannered. His behaviour with others at home and in the society is always pleasant. He/She is welcomed everywhere. People like the company of such a person. That is the reason why there is so much emphasis on learning good manners. People judge a person by his behaviour as we judge a tree by its leaves and fruit. A person of polished behaviour has better chances of success in life. A **polished** person finds all the doors open to him.

Childhood is the best age to learn good manners. He/She can very easily and quickly learn things and adapt himself/herself. It costs nothing to be good in our manners. It requires a strong will, discipline, self-control and desire to learn good manners. A truly educated person will always be well-mannered.

Know These Words

upbringing	-	the way a child is treated and taught how to behave
charm	-	a quality that attracts people
courtesy	-	polite behaviour
polished	-	refined

Questions-Answers

A. Fill in the blanks:–

1. __________ reveal a person's upbringing.
2. We should not hurt anyone by our __________ and __________.
3. Good manners represent the __________ and __________ progress of the society.
4. A well-mannered person always behaves __________ with everyone.
5. People judge a person by his/her __________.
6. Good manners are the other side of __________ and __________.

B. Answer the following questions:–

1. What do good manners reveal about a person?

____

2. Who is a well-mannered person?

____

3. 'Courtesy begets courtesy'. Explain.

____

4. On what basis do we judge a tree and a human being?

____

5. What is the best age to learn good manners?

____

6. What qualities are required to learn good manners?

____

Creative Writing

C. How do you present yourself in the society as a well-mannered person?

____

____

D. What is the importance of good manners in our life?

____

____

Word Power

E. Find the words (given in the Word Bank on the next page) in the word grid.

o	p	a	r	d	e	w	f	a	i	r	n	e	s	s
b	e	t	s	a	j	t	i	l	p	e	o	f	m	l
f	r	i	e	n	d	s	h	i	p	s	o	r	w	t
m	s	a	l	c	a	t	r	e	s	p	e	c	t	u
r	e	b	f	c	e	w	r	t	s	o	o	w	n	i
q	v	m	d	c	i	t	i	z	e	n	s	h	i	p
l	e	k	i	u	t	l	v	e	a	s	l	a	e	t
t	r	u	s	t	w	o	r	t	h	i	n	e	s	s
e	a	w	c	r	y	b	e	m	n	b	l	o	e	r
b	n	y	i	v	g	r	l	k	e	i	h	a	d	j
u	c	j	p	a	b	x	e	b	g	c	o	v	w	a
y	e	o	l	b	h	i	c	a	r	i	n	g	p	h
m	g	n	i	l	g	m	e	a	h	t	r	t	l	o
w	h	e	n	h	o	n	e	s	t	y	g	o	u	i
a	u	w	e	q	j	u	c	o	u	r	a	g	e	t

Word Bank

respect	caring	responsibility	fairness	perseverance	honesty
friendship	citizenship	trustworthiness	courage	self-discipline	

Grammar Skills

Types of a Subordinate Clause

Subordinate Clause → Noun Clause | Adjective Clause | Adverb Clause

Noun clause

The clause which acts as a noun in a sentence is called a Noun Clause.

For example : David knew that he would qualify.

1 2

David knew is the main clause. **that he would qualify** is the subordinate noun clause as it answers the question **what**?

A noun clause can act as the subject or the object or the complement of the verb or the object of the preposition in a sentence.

Adjective clause

The clause that acts as an adjective in a sentence is called an adjective clause. It describes the noun of the main clause.

It begins with a relative pronoun – that, who, which, whom or whose.

It also begins with a relative adverb – when, where or why.

Examples : 1. The girl who came today is my sister.

The girl is my sister — Main clause

Who came today — Adjective clause

2. The boy whom you know is my friend.

The boy is my friend — Main clause

Whom you know — Adjective clause

3. The girl whose mother is a teacher has come here.

The girl has come here — Main clause

Whose mother is a teacher — Adjective clause

Adverb clause

An adverb clause describes the verb in the subordinate clause. It acts like an adverb in a sentence.

Example : I came **when students were about to leave**.

Main clause (I came) — Adverb Clause (when students were about to leave)

F. Complete the conversation using the word who, which or that.

Sophia : Didn't you want to buy a new dress?

Ema : Yes, but not from this shop. Their choice is limited and I am not one of those people (1) ________ will buy anything that comes along.

Sophia : There's another shop over there.

Ema : It looks expensive; it is one of those places (2) _______ charge very high prices.

The only customers (3) _________ can afford their prices are the rich women (4) _______ do not mind spending lavishly.

Anyway, I can see a board (5) _________ says "FIXED PRICE". But I'm not going into a shop (6) _______ doesn't allow me bargaining.

Sophia : Well, what about this shop?

Ema : Oh! I don't like the look of the shop.

Sophia : My God! You are one of those people _______ are never satisfied, are you?

G. Complete the information in these news items. Make the sentences in the brackets into adjective clauses. Begin the sentences with 'The':

Example : A boy has won a trip to Goa.

(He won the story-writing contest.)

The boy who won the story-writing contest has won a trip to Goa.

1. An old man and a woman lived in this house before we did. (They wrote this book.)
2. A student was banned from taking the exam. (He cheated.)
3. A young man has just arrived. (He wants to meet my father.)

4. A famous library is situated in this city. (It was inaugurated by our Principal.)

5. A spaceship is on display here. (It landed on Mars.)

Let Us Know More

Good manners are very important in our daily life. Good manners are required to create an effective interaction with everyone as well as to make a good impression on them. It helps us to remain positive throughout the day. Good manners help a person to show the same character, both in front of and behind the people. The words and behaviour of a good-mannered person never change and remain the same in all conditions. Well-mannered persons know very well as to how to show or explain the bitter truth with sweet words and tone. The people who lack good manners generally have sharp and clear tongues. Bad people always behave roughly and abuse others without any reason. They show and pretend to be good in the society, but they are hated everywhere. Good-mannered people are welcomed everywhere.

Fun Chat

Read the quote and understand.

'Good manners will open doors that the best of education cannot'.

11 Childhood

When did my childhood go?
Was it the day I **ceased** to be eleven.
Was it the time I **realised** that
Hell and **heaven**,could not be found
in Geography, was that the day!

When did my childhood go?
Was it the time I realised that
Adults were not all they seemed to be,
They talked of love and **preached** of love,
But did not act so lovingly,
Was that the day!

When did my childhood go?
Was it when I found my mind
Was really mine,to use whichever
Way I choose, producing thoughts
That were not those other people
But my own and mine alone
Was that the day!

Where did my childhood go?
It went to some forgotten place,
That's hidden in an infant's face.
That's all I know.

Know These Words

ceased	-	came or brought to an end
realised	-	became fully aware of a fact
hell	-	the place where the Devil lives, and where wicked people are sent to be punished when they die.
heaven	-	a place where God lives and where good people go when they die
preached	-	publicly proclaimed or taught

Questions-Answers

A. Complete the sentences on the basis of your reading.

1. The poet wonders if it was the time when he crossed the age of eleven or the time when he started realising that ______________

____

____

____

____

2. The poet wonders if he lost his childhood, the moment he realised that adults

____

____

____

____

3. Or when he recognised that the adult, who ______________________________

____

____

____

____

4. The poet asks if he lost his childhood the moment he has a mind of his own or ____________

____

____

____

____

B. A child's life is peaceful whereas an adult's life is very complicated.

Write five qualities of each a child and an adult.

Child	Adult
____________	____________
____________	____________
____________	____________
____________	____________

C. What did the poet realise when he was twelve years Old?

____

____

D. Why did the poet think that he had lost his childhood?

____

____

E. Where does the poet find his lost childhood? How can he get it back?

____

____

Creative Writing

F. Write one of your childhood memories you like the most.

____

____

____

____

Word Power

G. Make as many words as you can, with the given words:

Friendship	Happiness

Grammar Skills

Adverbs

An adverb is a word that modifies the meaning of a verb, an adjective, or another adverb, *e.g;* boldly, slowly, etc.

H. Complete the sentences with the appropriate adverbs.

slowly	beautifully	carelessly	easily
excitedly	finally	suddenly	quickly

1. Come here _____________ . You have to see this !
2. We knew that she had got the job when we saw her _________ talking on the phone.
3. He __________ put the vase on the table. It fell to the floor.
4. Let's walk ___________. I don't want to be the first one at the meeting.
5. Sophia is throwing a party on Saturday. She ___________ finished her Ph.D.
6. Alexender __________ put up the bookshelves. It was too difficult for me to do on my own.
7. Everything happened so ____________ that we had to move to California in less than a month.
8. I was so surprised. His new apartment was ______________ decorated.

Let Us Know More

Childhood is the happiest period in every individual's life. During this period a person has no responsibilities or obligation. Every problem seems to be simple to solve, unlike in adulthood. Childhood is the time a person spends as a kid; it is full of fun. A child's life is free from all responsibilities and challenge of adulthood. His/Her mind is simple. He/She doesn't need wealth, precious things and elegant clothes. What exactly he/she needs is a happy family. Children believe in Santa, fairy tales and magic. They never think about what people think; they just do what they like. They don't live with the competitive life adults live. Every person thinks of the days when he/she was young. No one can deny that it was the happiest time in his/her life.

Fun Chat

Read the quote and understand

"When we are children, we seldom think of future. This innocence leaves us free to enjoy ourselves as few adults can. The day we grumble about future is the day we leave our childhood behind."

12 The Farmer and the Snake

Once upon a time, there was a farmer who used to go to his **farmyard** every morning for **harvesting** crops. Season after season, he followed this routine. At times the farmer would take his son along with him. Once, the farmer rose early in the morning and after a cup of steaming tea, he left for his farmyard along with his son. Both of them were **shivering** with cold though they had wrapped themselves with sweaters and mufflers. Suddenly, they saw a snake lying on the road. It was feeling so cold that it could hardly move. The farmer and his son felt pity for it.

The farmer took the snake in his lap. Instead of going to the farmyard, they came back to their residence.

The farmer then took the snake near a fire-place and kept it there for some minutes. Gradually, the snake became fresh and started moving inside the room. The farmer, fully aware of its **instinct**, kept distance from it. **Simultaneously**, he was thinking of the fact that the snake might spare them since they had saved its life. So, he assured his son and the other members of his family about the harmlessness of that snake. The snake became a pet. It was offered milk and bananas. Every day, when its meal was over, it used to go back to a nearby jungle and reappear the next day for meal.

One morning, after the snake had come for food, it saw the son of the farmer. It asked the farmer's son, "Come; let us play together." The farmer's son replied, "No, I don't have enough time to play. I'am going to the farmyard with my father." The snake got sad after its request was rejected by the farmer's son.

Remembering their help on a wintry morning, the snake controlled itself and requested the farmer's son again to play with him. This time also, the farmer's son replied in the negative. Now, the snake could not control itself. It was very angry with the farmer's son; hence, it tried to bite him. The farmer's son was frightened and reported it to his father. "We saved you from the cold and offered you food. But you tried to bite my son. You **ungrateful** fellow! Now you don't have any right to live here," the farmer said to the snake and killed it with a stick and returned to his residence.

Know These Words

farmyard	-	an area surrounded by farm buildings
harvesting	-	the cutting and collecting crops from the fields
shivering	-	shaking slightly as a result of being cold
instinct	-	the way people or animals naturally react
simultaneously	-	at the same time
ungrateful	-	not showing any thankfulness

Questions-Answers

A. Underline the correct answer.

1. Where did the farmer go every morning?
    a. Morning walk
    b. For his job
    c. Farmyard
    d. None of the above

2. What did farmer and his son see on the road?

a. A crocodile
b. A frog
c. An ant
d. A snake

3. The farmer took the snake to a–

a. fire-place
b. hospital
c. farmyard
d. friend's house

4. What did the farmer offer to the snake?

a. Biscuits and water
b. Milk and biscuits
c. Bananas and milk
d. Water and bananas

5. The snake was killed with–

a. a stick
b. a knife
c. a bat
d. None of the above

6. What is the moral of the story?

a. Always help everyone, no matter whatever the outcome can be.
b. Never trust anyone
c. Never feel pity on a scoundrel
d. Never say 'No' to anyone

B. Answer the following questions.

1. Why did the farmer go to the farmyard every day?

____

____

____

2. What did the farmer and his son find on the road? What happened to it?

____

____

____

3. How did the farmer treat the snake?

____

____

____

4. How did the snake become fresh and moveable inside the room?

____

____

____

5. What did the snake ask the farmer's son? What did he reply to the snake?

____

____

____

6. How did the snake react after the farmer's son had replied in the negative?

____

____

____

7. What did the farmer do with the snake?

____

____

____

Creative Writing

C. How would you react when you come across a wild insect or animal? How will you deal with this kind of situation? Write in your own words.

____

____

____

____

____

____

____

____

D. 'Pity those who really deserve to be pitied'. What is the meaning of this statement?

____

____

____

____

____

____

____

Word Power

E. Find the given words in the word grid.

b	a	p	a	b	h	s	p	i	t	m	t	l	e	a	a	d
e	d	o	d	e	y	t	r	z	q	o	y	e	a	e	t	a
e	r	n	e	e	r	a	t	e	u	s	u	a	r	o	s	m
t	r	d	f	p	x	g	s	d	g	q	i	f	w	p	f	s
l	d	s	g	d	i	b	q	s	y	u	o	h	i	a	j	e
e	o	k	t	s	y	e	i	d	p	i	p	o	g	p	f	l
a	a	a	u	s	p	e	o	u	s	t	a	p	z	e	d	f
s	n	t	i	y	i	t	p	t	y	o	e	p	e	r	t	l
t	t	e	o	u	o	l	u	d	m	a	t	e	o	w	z	y
x	p	r	p	i	l	e	x	s	o	t	u	r	d	a	h	d
y	i	o	s	d	a	e	t	i	t	i	z	r	l	s	i	a
a	m	b	u	s	h	b	u	g	h	k	o	o	f	p	l	e
c	o	c	k	r	a	o	a	c	h	u	o	p	u	o	x	p
t	l	a	c	e	w	i	n	g	a	s	e	t	i	o	v	u
b	e	d	b	u	g	v	s	t	i	n	k	b	u	g	y	e
t	a	u	i	p	o	y	h	o	v	e	r	f	l	y	u	d
v	c	r	i	c	k	e	t	d	f	a	d	h	g	a	c	d

prisoner	favour	good	prophet	poor
ambushbug	ant	aphid	bedbug	bee
beetle	cockroach	cricket	damselfly	earwig
gypsymoth	hoverfly	lacewing	leafhopper	mosquito
paperwasp	pondskater	stagbeetle	stinkbug	

Word Bank

Grammar Skills

Kinds of Adverbs

1. **Adverbs of Manner**

These show how or in **what manner** an action is done.

For example :

a. The soldiers fought **bravely**.

b. I do work **carefully**.

2. **Adverbs of Place**

These show **where** an action is done.

For example :

a. There is nobody **around**.

b. The bus stops **there**.

3. **Adverbs of Time**

These show **when** an action is done.

For example :

a. They will be **late**.

b. She reached here **yesterday**.

4. **Adverbs of Degree**

These show **how much** or to **what extent** a thing is done.

For example :

a. I am **quite** tired now.

b. I am **fully** prepared.

5. Adverbs of Frequency

These show **how often** or **how many** times a thing is done.

For example :

a. He **never** gets late.

b. I **rarely** go to his place.

6. Interrogative Adverbs

These are used for **asking questions** about **place, time, manner, reason, number,** etc.

For example :

a. **How** is she today?

b. **Why** have you not completed your homework?

7. Conjunctive Adverbs

These join two clauses with a conjunction.

For example :

a. This is the reason **why** I left.

b. I will show you the place **where** we are constructing our house.

F. Underline the adverbs in the following sentences and state their kinds.

1. I went to the market yesterday. ______________
2. The dog sat lazily in the shade of the tree. ______________
3. The man grumbled loudly, while cleaning. ______________
4. I often visit my grandparents. ______________
5. It is extremely hot today. ______________
6. Please wait patiently. ______________
7. They serve hot pancakes there. ______________
8. He laugh merrily. ______________
9. The girls danced gracefully. ______________
10. She has travelled everywhere. ______________

Let Us Know More

Trust is important because it is the basis around which all relationships revolve. Trust can come naturally or it can be manifested through regular behaviour. Trust is fundamental to life. If you cannot trust anything, life will become intolerable. No one is perfect in this world and some people aren't trustworthy.

Whenever we trust another person, we face several risks. First of all, we may become dependent on that person, and we may start feeling a diminished sense of trust in ourselves. We've put such a huge part of our own burden on someone else that we may lose our own ability to deal with trails, troubles and difficulties.

Always remember these acts of kindness.

1. Smile.
2. Hold the door open while someone else is leaving or entering.
3. Give an honest compliment.
4. Thank someone who you appreciate.
5. Be a good listener.
6. Offer your help to someone.

Fun Chat

Some amazing facts about snakes :

1. Snakes Evolved 142 Million Years Ago
2. They Have Unique Skeletons
3. They Can Drink Water Without Lips
4. They Can Survive For Months Without Eating
5. Snakes Do Not Have Eyelids
6. Snakes Do Not Have External Ears – But Can Still Hear

13 Tale of Three Fishes

Once upon a time, there lived three fishes among many other fish in a pond. One day, some fishermen were passing by the pond. They examined the pond and found that the pond was full of fish.

Since they were returning after catching fish, and already had a big **haul**, they decided to come back the next morning.

They discussed, “This pond is full of fish and there are many big ones too. We have never caught fish in this pond. Let us come back tomorrow morning.”

The three fishes were swimming on the surface when they heard the fishermen discussing their plan.

The first fish **panicked**. He immediately **assembled** all the other fishes and told them what he had heard. He said, “Tomorrow morning, the fishermen will arrive to catch us. I do not want to die like this. So, I will leave with my family at the earliest. I advise all of you to follow me. It will not be wise for anybody to stay here any longer.”

The second fish agreed, “I shall follow you, my friend, for what you say is correct. It will be unwise to remain here any more!”

But the third fish disagreed and mocked at them. She said to the fish assembled, "See how **cowardly** these two act! This pond belongs to our **forefathers**, and it is our home. For so long, no harm has ever been done to the fish of this pond. Just because some fishermen were discussing their plan, it is no reason for us to panic and leave our home. Those who agree with me, I advise them to stay here and not to go to some unknown place."

He further said, "O Friends, the **scriptures** state that when the time for one's death arrives, no one is spared. If death has to come, let us rather die bravely in our home!"

Thus, the fish of the pond got divided into two groups. The group that wanted to stay **mocked** at the other group. However, by evening, the families of the first two fishes started their journey to a different pond through a small outlet. They were followed by many other fish who believed in them.

The next morning, the fishermen arrived as per their plan and trapped all the fishes that remained in the pond by casting their nets all over the pond.

Not a single fish was spared, and the fishermen were overjoyed with the big haul of fish that they had caught.

Know These Words

haul	-	drag; pull
panicked	-	terrified; scared
assembled	-	gathered together in one place for a common purpose
cowardly	-	lacking courage
forefathers	-	ancestors
mocked	-	teased or laughed at someone

Questions-Answers

A. Underline the correct answer.

1. What did the fisherman examine in the pond?
   a. That the pond is full of fish
   b. A crocodile in the pond
   c. A boy drowning in the pond
   d. None of the above

2. Who all left the pond?
   a. The first and the third fish left
   b. The second and the third fish left
   c. The first and the second fish left
   d. All three fishes left their home

3. Who heard the fishermen's conversation?
   a. Third fish
   b. First fish
   c. Second fish
   d. All the three fishes

4. What is the moral of the story?
   a. Never laugh at anyone
   b. Never help anyone
   c. Always think of your own self
   d. Act wisely when there arises a problem

B. Answer the following questions.

1. What did the fishermen discuss?

____

____

____

2. Who did the first fish assemble and what did he tell them?

____

____

____

3. Why did the third fish mock at the other two fishes?

____

____

____

4. What did the third fish further say?

____

____

____

5. Where did the first two fishes start their journey?

6. What did the fishermen do the next morning?

7. Why were the fishermen overjoyed?

Creative Writing

C. How should we act, when we sense any danger?

Word Power

D. Complete the following crossword puzzle with the words using the hints on the next page.

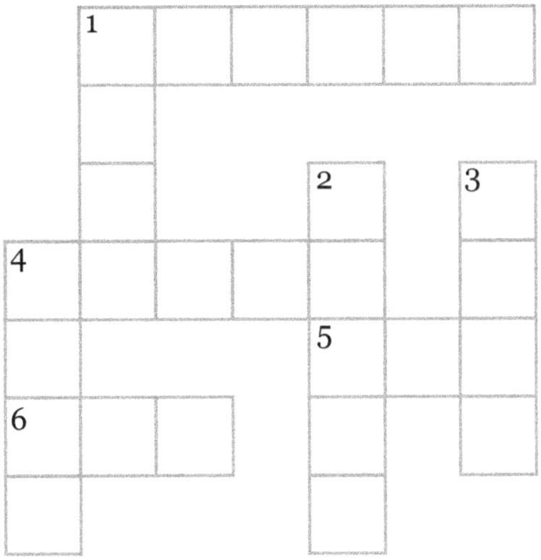

Word Bank

net, sea, fish, sink, follow, Jesus, boat, shore

Across

1. To get behind someone and go where he/she goes
4. The land along the edge of an ocean, a sea, lake or river
5. A large area of salty water, smaller than an ocean
6. An openwork fabric of cords used for catching fish

Down

1. An animal which lives in water and is covered with scales
2. The son of God
3. A small vehicle for travelling on water
4. To go down below the surface of the water

Grammar Skills

Adjectives

The words that give more information about nouns or pronouns and can go in different positions in sentences are called adjectives.

For example : 1. They live in a **big, beautiful** house.
2. The mountain-tops are covered in **sparkling** snow.
3. She wore a **beautiful** dress.

E. Underline the adjectives in the given sentences:

1. There I met a very beautiful woman.
2. He was wearing a red shirt.
3. The rich woman is known for her generosity.
4. The old man has seen better days.
5. Iron is a useful metal.
6. It was a good offer; I could not refuse it.
7. He died a glorious death.
8. A small leak is enough to sink a great ship.
9. That woman has curly hair.
10. He spoke harsh words to me.

Let Us Know More

It is good to know that we can always choose what we will do with the advice people give us.

1. We can take it.
2. We can ignore it.
3. We can ponder over it.
4. We can analyse it.
5. We can let it inspire us.
6. We can take only part of it and ignore the rest.
7. We can agree to it.
8. We can disagree to it.
9. We can question it.
10. We can modify it.

We need to remember that we are never under an obligation to take/apply it but we must consider the good advice once.

Fun Chat

Read and understand the quote.

'Nothing is a waste of time if you use the experience wisely.'

14 Importance of Books

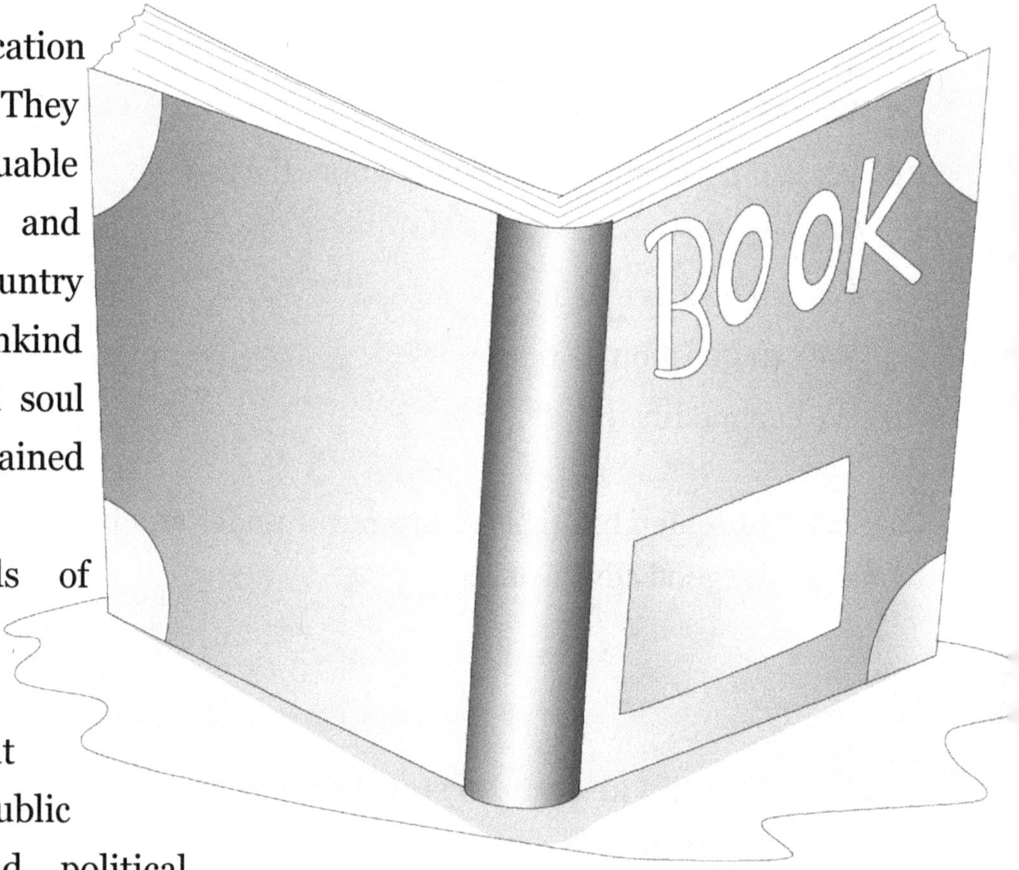

Good books are the Education Master of the world. They impart knowledge and valuable instructions to mankind and make the citizens of a country worthy. The entire mankind uplifts its body, mind and soul through the knowledge gained from good books.

There are various kinds of books available in the market. Some of the books written on important subjects like economics, public administration, civics and political science, make a person understand the social and economic structure of the world. The person also comes to realise his rights and duties as the citizen of a country through books. Some of the **autobiographies** of great personalities give us great lessons and we learn to correct our own mistakes after knowing the **consequences** of our wrong deeds from the experiences of great leaders.

For instance, if any leader has suffered the bad experience of any wrong act, we can know the result of that action and will never act the same way. Some books are written by judicious psychologists, who teach us to judge the personalities of the people through various gestures. Understanding the psychology of people can eliminate many misunderstandings caused among friends, relatives and other relations, and improve the relations among them.

Books not only **enhance** our knowledge in various fields but also are a good source of entertainment. We can read and enjoy them in our journeys. We can go through good books in our bedrooms, drawing rooms or whenever we have some spare time. As the pages of a book are turned over, a child's word power is broadened. In the same manner, literature is equally valuable and important for many reasons. It enhances children's imagination; introduces them to new people, places and ideas; builds their vocabulary and strengthens the use of language; and simplifies difficult tasks with simple solutions.

Books also enhance the love between parents and children. Some children love to snuggle up to their parents for soulful bedtime stories.

So, children should be exposed to quality books of all kinds, be it picture, story, rhythm and rhyming, adventure and mystery, fantasy, inter-personal relationship, travel, reference, riddle and puzzle, art and science. Reading will become a treasured part of child's life. Books are our best companions; we can take their help to answer all the queries of our minds and satiate our thirst of knowledge.

Know These Words

autobiograph(y) ies - account of a person's life written by himself/herself

consequences - results

enhance - increase

Questions-Answers

A. Complete the following sentences:

1. Good books are the ____________________ of the world.
2. Understanding the psychology of people can ____________________ and ____________________
3. Books are a good source of ____________.
4. Literature enhances children's ____________, introduces them to new people and ____________ and ____________ with simple solutions.
5. Books are the best companions as we could take their help to answer ____________ and ____________.
6. Some children love to snuggle up to their parents for ____________ ____________________.

B. Answer the following questions.

1. What do good books impart to mankind?

2. What can the entire mankind gather through good books?

3. How are the autobiographies of great personalities helpful to us? What do we learn from them?

4. How are books a good source of entertainment?

5. How is literature valuable?

6. How do books enhance the love between parents and children?

7. How will reading become a treasured part of a child's life?

Creative Writing

C. What is the importance of books in our life?

D. What kind of books do you prefer to read?

____

____

____

Word Power

E. Find the words (given in the Word Bank on the next page) in the word grid.

b	d	x	r	t	s	b	n	m	w	u	i	r	a	t	c	t	t
e	b	o	y	d	u	m	p	l	i	n	g	g	n	o	l	h	o
a	f	r	t	g	s	r	t	t	n	i	r	f	g	i	a	e	b
u	d	s	h	a	p	i	g	h	n	s	e	b	e	l	r	w	e
t	d	a	e	d	e	f	g	e	i	d	e	a	l	u	a	o	a
y	d	v	l	e	t	i	o	i	e	l	n	k	i	y	c	r	k
a	x	l	i	o	n	f	i	s	t	p	e	e	n	l	t	l	i
n	t	c	t	b	b	n	w	l	h	l	g	t	b	u	h	d	d
d	y	r	t	b	o	t	f	a	e	h	g	l	e	y	e	o	b
t	d	t	l	f	t	d	j	n	p	r	s	s	i	t	s	l	n
h	t	b	e	t	f	i	s	d	o	b	a	t	j	c	n	c	m
e	d	t	p	u	d	g	u	o	o	p	n	a	i	y	o	i	l
b	t	f	r	v	d	s	y	f	h	d	d	r	n	h	w	t	b
e	a	m	i	i	r	e	s	q	u	i	h	b	g	p	y	i	t
a	s	f	n	o	g	f	i	s	h	o	a	t	y	c	d	e	t
s	l	o	c	f	i	s	h	d	t	g	m	z	u	d	a	s	s
t	b	a	e	k	e	t	s	t	a	r	t	y	d	r	y	t	t
t	h	e	s	e	c	r	e	t	k	i	n	g	d	o	m	t	o

Word Bank			
	Boy Dumpling	Angel in Beijing	Clara
	A World of Cities	The Secret Kingdom	To Be a kid
	The Snowy Day	Beauty and the Beast	Green Eggs and Ham
	Winnie the Pooh	The Little Prince	

Grammar Skills

Comparison of Adjectives

Adjectives have three degrees of comparison.

Positive Degree

It indicates 'no comparison' between two nouns or pronouns. For example : a **tall** boy, a **fat** man, a **thin** girl

Comparative Degree

It indicates 'comparison' between two nouns or pronouns. For example: **taller** boy, **fatter** man, **thinner** girl

Superlative Degree

It indicates 'comparison' **between more than two nouns or pronouns**'. For example : the **tallest** boy in the class, the **fattest** man in the colony, the **thinnest** girl in the family

F. Fill in the blanks with the suitable degrees of adjectives of quality given in the brackets.

1. Elizer is the ___________ student in our class. (good)
2. Jackson is the ___________ person in the entire office. (busy)
3. The pen is ___________ than the sword. (mighty)
4. He is as ___________ as his father. (handsome)
5. The pond is not so ___________ as it appears. (shallow)
6. This wall is too ___________ to climb. (high)
7. I found Maths very ___________; in fact, it is the ___________ of all the subjects. (difficult)

Let Us Know More

Books play an important role in our life. It is said that books are our best companions. They demand nothing from us, instead they give us plenty of joy and knowledge. We also learn a lot from them. They take us into a different world of imagination. Reading good books has many advantages. Good books build characters. They ignite the passion of humanity in the mind of the reader. But we should be very careful in selecting books. Good books develop good qualities in us, whereas bad books pervert our minds. Good books, magazines and journals dispel boredom from our life and make our life happier. Only a sincere reader of good books knows what divine pleasure he/she gets from reading books.

Fun Chat

Riddle Time

Guess the answers to the given riddles.

1. 2 painters can paint two rooms in two hours. How many painters would paint 18 rooms in 6 hours?
2. Which building has the most stories?

15 The Fallen Leaves

Why should I be the first to fall
Of all the leaves on this old tree?
Though sadly soon I know that all
Will lose their hold and follow me.
While my birth-brothers bravely blow
Why should I be the first to go?

Why should I be the last to cling
Of all the leaves on this **bleak bough**?
I've fluttered since the fire of Spring
And I am worn and **withered** now
I would escape the Winter **gale**
And sleep soft-silvered by a snail.

When **swoop** the legions of the snow
To pitch their tent in roaring weather
We fallen leaves will lie below
And **rot** rejoicingly together.
And from our rich and dark decay
Will laugh our brothers of the May.

Know These Words

bleak	-	charmless
bough	-	branch
withered	-	dry and decaying
gale	-	a very strong wind
swoop	-	drop
legions	-	very large in number
rot	-	decay

Questions-Answers

A. On the basis of your reading of the above poem, complete the summary of the poem given below, by filling in each blank with a word or a phrase.

In the first stanza, a fallen leaf laments its fate because it is the (a)________________ to fall while all its (b)________________are still attached to the tree. In the second stanza, another leaf still (c) ________________ to the branch of the same tree expresses its grief because it has still not (d) ______________down. It has been fluttering since (e)________________ and feels quite (f)______________ now. It is dying to fall off so that it may go to (g)________________. It's looking forward to the approaching (h) ________________ which will cover both the trees and the (i) ________________ with snow. Then all the fallen leaves will rejoice together as they (j) ______________________. Finally, from this soil will rise the fresh (k)__________________ in (l)________________________.

B. On the basis of your reading of the above poem, complete the following statements.

1. The bough has been described as "bleak" because–

   ____

   ____

2. Explain the meaning of the last two lines of the poem.

   ____

   ____

Creative Writing

C. **Have you ever observed trees in the seasons of autumn and spring season? What difference do you find in both seasons?**

____

____

D. **How do you feel when all your friends leave you alone and go on a fun tour without you?**

____

____

Word Power

E. **Complete the crossword puzzle using the hints.**

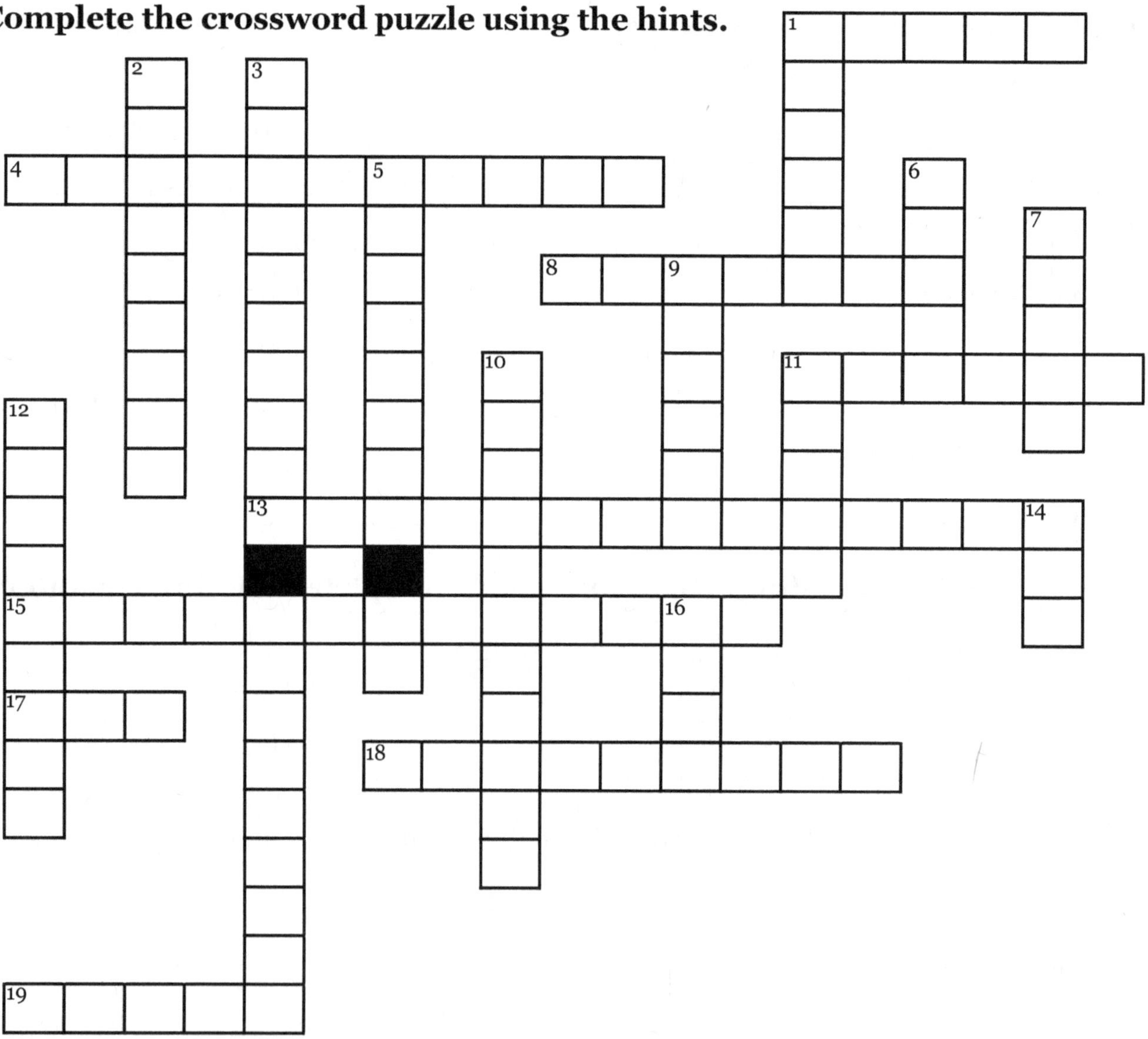

Across

1. the product of photosynthesis
4. process by which carbon circulates around the earth as plants remove carbon from the atmosphere and animals add carbon to the atmosphere
8. specialized structure that allows gas to enter and leave the leaf
11. part of the plant where photosynthesis generally occurs
13. the process by which plants and some bacteria use the energy from sunlight to produce sugar
15. a compound needed for photosynthesis
17. molecule used for storing energy
18. flattened sacs or vesicles containing photosynthetic chemicals
19. chlorophyll absorbs every colour of sunlight except this

Down

1. place where dark reactions occur
2. an animal that eats plants
3. the process of converting energy from a light-excited electron into the pyrophosphate bond of an ADP molecule
5. a group of accessory pigments that include beta-carotene
6. place where light reaction occurs
7. a compound needed for photosynthesis
9. a by-product of photosynthesis
10. a plant pigment that absorbs sunlight
11. this reaction requires direct energy of sunlight to make energy-carrier molecules
12. the links between the energy that carnivores get from eating to the energy captured by photosynthesis
14. number of molecules of oxygen produced along with one molecule sugar
16. reaction that occurs when the products of the Light Reaction are used for forming CC equivalent bond of carbohydrates

Grammar Skills

Prepositions

A preposition is a word which is used before a noun or pronoun to tell its relation with some other words in the sentence.

For example :

1. The book is **on** the table.
2. The pen is **in** the pocket.

Therefore, the words 'on' and 'in' are prepositions. Each of them links the two nouns.

Kind of Prepositions

1. Simple Prepositions

These prepositions are in simple form.

For example :

The chair is made **of** wood.

The cow is **in** the field.

2. Compound Prepositions

A compound preposition contains two or more prepositional words.

For example :

Robbers were travelling **without** tickets.

The noise came **from across** the river.

3. Phrase Prepositions

A phrase which consists of a simple preposition at the end and is used like a preposition is called a phrase preposition.

For example :

She acted **according to** instructions.

F. Fill in the blanks with the appropriate prepositions:

1. I cannot think ________ teasing an animal.
2. He is working ________ the university.
3. I told you ________ a boy yesterday.
4. The box was full ________ money.
5. The book is ________ no use _______ me.

6. I thank all of you __________ my parents.
7. She came to the party ________ her mother.
8. What are you looking ________?
9. Please get ________ the roof.
10. The hunter aimed ________ the bird.
11. The room is heated ________ an electric heater.
12. She is down ________ fever.
13. The boat was sailing ________ the river.
14. The boy is walking ________ the park.
15. The baby crawled ________ me.

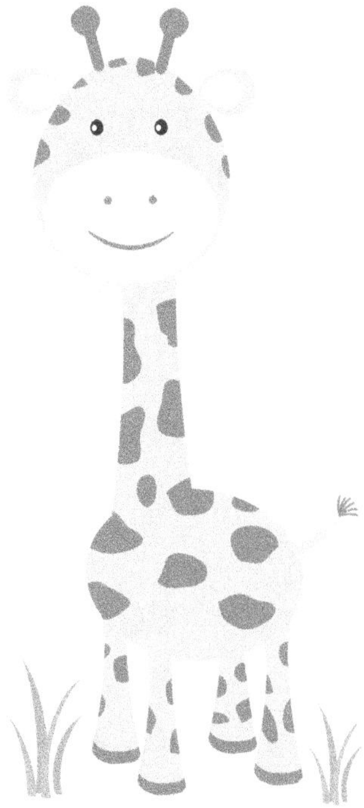

G. Rewrite the following sentences using the correct prepositions.

1. Joseph is slow with English.

____

____

2. I am tired at false excuses.

____

____

3. Let's hope of the best.

____

____

4. I did it in your good.

____

____

5. The milk is on the glass.

____

____

Let Us Know More

When the fallen leaves decay, it makes humus, and this humus is a very important thing to have in the soil. The roots of the tree continually bring up mineral salts from the subsoil, and a certain amount of these valuable salts is left behind in the leaves when they fall. The tree which makes preparation for winter, has no further use for these salts, which are merely the raw materials for its thousands of little food factories, the leaves.

Fun Chat

Riddle Time

I'm sometimes big
And sometimes small
In autumn
You see me fall
I can be blown but I'm not a bubble.
I drop but I'm not a tear
I come in different shapes but I'm not a snowflake.
I come in different colours but I'm not a cellphone
I come from a tree but I'm not an apple.

16 The Cobra and the Crows

There was a big banyan tree, where two crows husband and wife, had built a nice nest and lived happily. In the **hollow** of the same tree, lived a black cobra. The crows had a problem because the black cobra would climb up the tree and eat the newborns, whenever the female crow hatched her eggs. They could do absolutely nothing to save them.

The crows went to a jackal, who lived in a nearby banyan tree, to seek his advice. They narrated everything to him and sought his advice to get rid of their problem.

They said, "O Friend, it has become dangerous to live here. Please tell us how we can protect our children from being eaten up by the **wicked** black cobra."

The jackal replied, "Please don't give up. Even powerful enemies can be overcome with the use of wit."

On hearing this, the crows requested, "O Friend, please tell us how we can overcome and destroy this wicked cobra."

The jackal told them a plan, “Fly into the capital of the kingdom, not far from here. Visit the house of someone who is wealthy and careless. Notice if something valuable is lying around. If you find so, pick it up when the servants are watching you.”

He continued, “You will need to fly slowly so that the servants may follow you. Return to your tree and drop it in the hollow of the tree where the cobra lives. When the servants reach, they will kill the cobra when they see it.”

The crows decided to follow the jackal’s advice and flew off immediately according to his plan.

As they flew above the capital, the female crow noticed wealthy women swimming in a lake. They had left gold and pearl necklaces on the banks of the lake, which were being guarded by the royal servants.

At once, the female crow **swooped** down and picked up a big necklace in her beak and started flying slowly.

When the royal servants noticed her, they picked up sticks and stones, and started throwing at her and chased her.

As planned, she dropped the necklace in front of the hollow of the tree, where the black cobra was asleep. She sat on one of the branches for the royal servants to notice.

When the royal servants arrived, the black cobra came out of the hollow of the tree to see what all the noise was about. The black cobra **confronted** the king’s servants with swelling hood, but the servants attacked the cobra with sticks and stones to recover the necklace.

They killed the wicked cobra and returned with the necklace. And the crows, having got rid of the cobra, lived happily.

Know These Words

hollow	-	empty space in a tree
wicked	-	morally wrong
swooped	-	moved very quickly
confronted	-	challenged

Questions-Answers

A. Underline the correct answer.

1. What was the relationship between two crows who lived on the banyan tree?

   a. Brother and sister　　b. Husband and wife

   c. Mother and father　　d. None of the above

2. The two crows and a cobra lived on the ________ tree.

   a. Rubber tree　　b. Ashoka tree

   c. Banyan tree　　d. Banana tree

3. The crows went to the ________ to seek his advice.

   a. To their friends　　b. To their elders

   c. Jackal　　d. To the black cobra

4. Did the crows decide to follow the jackal's advice?

   a. Yes　　b. No

5. What did the female crow steal?

   a. A ring　　b. A necklace

   c. An ear-ring　　d. A shoe

6. Where did the female crow drop the necklace?

   a. On the door

   b. In the nest

   c. In front of the hollow of the banyan tree

   d. In the garden

B. Answer the following questions.

1. Who lived on the banyan tree?

   ____

   ____

2. What problem did the crows have?

   ____

   ____

3. Where did the crows go to seek advice?

4. What did the jackal reply?

5. What did the female crow notice?

6. What did the female crow do after seeing the gold and pearl necklaces?

7. Where did she drop the necklace?

8. Who did the servants attack and kill?

Creative Writing

C. How do you think an enemy can be overcome - by wisdom or by physical war?

D. Can you share any one experience of yours where you used your wit and wisdom to win a game?

____

____

____

____

____

____

Word Power

E. Find the given words (in the Word Bank on the next page) in the word grid.

r	g	l	i	z	a	r	d	g	o	a	t	u	a
c	l	f	h	e	l	t	r	u	t	e	s	r	i
a	u	s	g	h	s	n	a	k	e	u	h	a	g
t	i	n	u	a	i	e	r	b	i	r	d	l	u
t	a	a	i	m	i	f	l	g	b	d	o	i	a
u	g	k	n	s	a	f	t	e	s	s	l	b	n
s	t	e	e	t	b	o	t	u	r	t	l	e	a
d	e	f	a	e	e	m	t	l	r	f	e	e	g
i	r	b	p	r	g	o	i	g	a	o	l	g	a
t	g	h	i	h	r	u	u	h	t	t	a	i	e
d	k	u	g	r	i	s	c	h	i	c	k	e	n
o	a	b	a	a	r	e	d	f	e	r	r	e	t
g	t	n	r	n	a	u	d	u	a	a	t	s	k
f	i	s	h	i	c	h	o	p	p	e	r	o	h

Word Bank					
cat	bird	chicken	iguana	fish	chopper
guinea pig	rat	dog	ferret	hamster	
lizard	snake	goat	turtle	mouse	

Grammar Skills

Present Continuous Tense

It is used for actions happening now or for an action that is unfinished. This is also used when the action is temporary. It follows the formula:

'be' verb [am, is, are......] + first form of verb + ing.

For example :

1. He **is driving** erratically.
2. They **are sitting** at the table.
3. We **are baking** a cake.

F. Fill in the blanks with the present continous tense:

1. The labourer ____________ (push) the cart.
2. He ____________ (flatter) the boss.
3. I ____________ (take) the examination in this month.
4. The police ____________ (catch) the thief.
5. They ____________ (play) badminton right now.
6. Jacob ____________ (play) the guitar.
7. I ____________ (iron) my clothes.
8. Mr William ____________ (take) the dose of medicine.

Let Us Know More

You will find problems in every action if it is against the law of Nature. If you take every obstacle or opposition as a problem, your life will become miserable. Every action requires certain amount of effort or intelligent approach and in the absence of it, one will note that any action, which is against the law of Nature, results in a problem. If you anticipate a problem, you must prepare well in advance to face the situation. Difficulty in performing a particular task is not a problem since it requires dedication and devotion. All problems should be analysed and proper action should be taken depending upon the nature of the problem.

Fun Chat

Read the jokes and laugh aloud.

Why did the maths book look so sad?

Because it had so many problems.

☺ ☺ ☺

Do you find English easy?

If yes, fill in each blank with Yes or No.

1. _______, I don't have a brain.
2. _______, I don't have sense.
3. _______, I am stupid.

☺ ☺ ☺

17 Public Relations

A man can never attain success in life, if he doesn't know how to keep **cordial** relations with the people around him. Though a man may be extraordinarily brilliant, smart, practical and **dynamic** yet he would not be able to achieve success if he fails to please people with whom he comes in contact with. Although it is a truth that one can't please all the people all the times, one can certainly please sensible people with the right kind of approach in life.

To please people, firstly, we should be down-to-earth and remain away from artificialities as well false pretensions of life. Thereafter, we should understand the **psychology** of people. Ask questions about them to know as well as understand their behaviour and their attitude towards life. What do they like to wear, eat or drink? What are their ambitions?

After gaining knowledge about them, talk or chat about their likes and dislikes. Listen to them more and talk less. Talk politely in a low tone so that they may not get irritated from your voice. Be humble enough to serve a plate or glass to your guest. People get attached to humbleness and want their company.

Never insult or **degrade** anyone around you. If you want to correct the faults of any person, then you should mention his qualities along with his flaws.

People don't feel insulted if you point their flaws with their qualities. Only condemning and degrading others in public is not good. We must realise that we too are human beings who can commit mistakes and, thus, nobody is perfect on this earth. One might be better than others, but, not perfect.

Even great leaders, writers, sportsmen and film stars are also not perfect. They may be better than others in understanding or **sensibility** but they may also commit mistakes in their life. Thus, it is not wise to expect perfection from a common man.

Therefore, we ought to correct our own flaws first before correcting others. This is the best way to improve our relationship with the people around us and to achieve success in life.

Know These Words

cordial	-	warm and friendly
dynamic	-	active; productive
psychology	-	study of mind
degrade	-	treat someone with disrespect
sensibility	-	ability to receive sensations

Questions-Answers

A. Underline the correct option.

1. A man must know how to keep _______________ with the people around him.
   a. permanent relations b. temporary relations
   c. cordial relations d. purposeful relations

2. **Which qualities of a man can lead him to achieve success?**
   a. Rude and honest nature b. Practical and dynamic nature
   c. Brillant and smart nature d. Both (b) and (c)

3. **What is the right kind of approach in life?**
   a. Please sensible people b. Please arrogant people
   c. Please rude people d. Please honest people

4. **People get attached to __________.**
   a. rudeness b. honesty
   c. humbleness d. none of the above

5. What should we do to correct others' faults?

a. Share your philosphical thoughts

b. Mention their flaws with their qualities

c. Mention their flaws

d. None of the above

B. Answer the following questions.

1. Who can never attain success in life and why?

____

____

2. What should we do to please people?

____

____

3. What should we do after gaining knowledge about the people around us?

____

____

4. Whom should we never insult or degrade and why?

____

____

5. What is not good?

____

____

6. What must we realise?

____

____

7. Who are not perfect?

____

____

8. What is the best way to improve the relationship with people and what we achieve?

____

____

Creative Writing

C. How do you behave with the people of your society?

____

____

____

____

____

D. Do you commit a mistake and how do you improve yourself after committing the mistake?

____

____

____

____

____

____

Word Power

E. Write one word for each of the following.

1. A person employed to organize advertising or publicity in the press on behalf of an organization is called a ________________.
2. Views prevalent among the general public are called __________.
3. Communication in which both parties involved transmit information is called ______________.
4. Conversation between two or more people about a book, play or movie is called _________________.

5. The quality of being crystal clear is called ______________.

6. Efforts, object of a person or ambition to achieve the desired results is called ______________________.

Grammar Skills

Present Perfect Tense

This tense is used for showing a link between the present and past and is commonly used in everyday conversation. It follows the formula of : Have/Has + past participle (III form of verb).

For example :

1. He **has coached** the team since 1998.
2. She **has broken** her arm twice.
3. The robbers **have stolen** over 16 cars and are still at large.

F. Put each verb in the correct Present Perfect form.

1. I ______________ (not/work) today.
2. We ______________ (buy) a new lamp.
3. We ______________ (not/plan) our holiday yet.
4. He ______________ (speak) to his boss.
5. No, he ______________ (not/get) the time yet.

G. Convert each into present perfect tense.

1. I study French.

____

2. She eats an octopus.

____

3. We read that book.

____

4. He lived here for three years.

____

5. They miss the train.

____

6. She goes to Peru.

____

7. You find your wallet.

____

8. She passed the exam.

____

Let Us Know More

Everyone must have good manners. A man is known by his manners. A man having good manners is appreciated everywhere. Good manners cannot be borrowed; they have to be cultivated and grown slowly. We should cultivate good manners from our early childhood since these are the integral part of a society or country. Good manners require voluntary obedience to certain codes of conduct, such as, we should never lose temper. We should be polite in our behaviour. We should not talk loudly to anyone.

Fun Chat

Read the joke and laugh aloud.

Young Jacob was having a snack after school with his Granny. "Would you like another cookie?" She asked.

"Yes, please," replied Jacob.

"What good manners do you have?" said his Granny,

"I do like to hear young people say 'please' and 'thank you'."

"I'll say them both if I can have a big piece of that cake," replied Jacob.

18 Breakfast

Of all the meals that glad my day
My morning one's the best;
Purveyed me on a silver tray,
Immaculately dressed.

I **rouse** when the dawn is bright,
I leap into the sea.
Returning with a **rare** delight
To honey, toast and tea.

My appetite was **razor-edged**
When I was in my prime;
To eggs and **bacon** I was **pledged**.
Ala ! The March of Time ;
For now a **genial** old **gent**
With journal on my knee,
I sip and take with vast content
My honey, toast and tea.

So set me up for my delight
The harvest of the bee;
with butter bright,
Brown, crispy toast
Ceylon-two cups or three.
Let others lunch or dinner **praise**,
But I **regale** with glee,
As I regard with grateful **gaze**,
Just honey, toast and tea.

Know These Words

purveyed	-	provided / supplied
immaculately	-	cleanly or tidily
rouse	-	wake up
rare	-	uncommon
razor-edged	-	extremely penetrating
bacon	-	meat from the side of a pig
pledged	-	committed
genial	-	cheerful; hospitable
gent	-	short for gentleman
Ceylon	-	tea
praise	-	appreciation
regale	-	entertain
gaze	-	a steady intent look

Questions-Answers

A. On the basis of your reading of the above poem, complete the summary of the poem, filling in the blanks with the missing words.

After returning from the (a) ______________, in the morning the poet experiences (b) ______________ in having breakfast which is the day's best meal comprising honey, toast and tea.

With time, the poet has transformed from a young man to an (c) ______________. Similarly, his taste has also changed from (d) ______________ to honey, toast and tea. The poet differs from others in that, while he thinks that breakfast is the (e) ______________ of the day, others may (f) ______________.

B. The poet uses certain expressions in the poem to suggest a few things to the reader. There are some suggestions given below in circles. Choose one suggestion that best fits each of the expressions in the table.

Expression from the poem	To suggest that
• Immaculately dressed	(a)
• My appetite was razor-edged	(b)
• March of Time	(c)
• Regard with grateful glee	(d)

perfectly laid out

passage of time

I was extremely hungry

respect and offer with happiness

Creative Writing

C. What do you do when you feel very hungry? How do you manage your appetite when you don't get something favourite to eat?

Word Power

D. Complete the following puzzle using the clues.

Across

6. the addition of nutrients to a food-item that were lost during processing.
7. sometimes known as "blood sugar"
8. a form of carbohydrate found in plant food that is not digested by the human digestive enzymes
9. chemical substance obtained from food and used in the body

10. condition caused by excess of deficient food energy or nutrient intake, or by an imbalance of nutrients

13. providing all of the essential nutrients, fibre and energy in sufficient amount to maintain health

14. found in meat, poultry, fish, eggs, milk, nuts and seeds

Down

1. the physiological drive for food
2. units by which energy is measured
3. eating a wide selection of food within and among the major food groups
4. higher than normal blood pressure
5. providing enough, but not too much, of a substance.
11. the body's ability to recognize and eliminate foreign invaders, such as bacteria
12. providing foods of a number of types in proportion to each other.

Grammar Skills

Past Continuous Tense

The past continuous tense is used for describing actions that began in the past. The formula for past continuous is:-

was/were + root verb (1st form) + ing

For example :

1. The sun **was shining** every day in summers.
2. I **was eating** dinner.

E. Fill in the blanks using past continuous Tense.

1. Julie was ___________ (sleep) at three o'clock.
2. Luke ___________ (read) a book.
3. They___________ (eat) chocolates.
4. He ___________ (use) his mobile phone.
5. You ___________ (cook) lunch.
6. The dogs ___________ (not/play) outside when the murder was committed.
7. I ___________ (not/listen) to music.

Let Us Know More

Breakfast is the most important meal of the day. There is an old saying "Eat breakfast like a king, lunch like a prince and dinner like a pauper" which stands very true today as well. We might not have time to have a lavish breakfast buffet spread like a king, but having even a healthy dish makes the difference. Breakfast literally means breaking the fast, since our body doesn't eat anything till we wake up in the next morning after a long sleep having consumed dinner last night. So, we should never skip breakfast.

Fun Chat

Riddle Time

1. What do snowmen like to eat for breakfast?
2. What can you never eat for breakfast?

19 Honesty

Long, long ago, there lived a king who was known for his truthfulness, charity and **valour**. Since the king was growing old, he decided to choose a **successor**. He had two sons and many relatives who could succeed him but he thought that they were not very honest. Therefore, he decided to select someone who had the quality of honesty.

One day, he asked the youth of his kingdom to gather in the Central Hall of the palace. He addressed them, "My dear children, I want to choose the next king who is the most capable so that the people of the country may be safe in his rule. I want to choose the person amongst you, who deserves the throne.

For this purpose, I have decided to give a test. I am handing over a seed to each of you. Each one of you has to keep the seed in a pot, **nurture** it and grow it into a plant. I will examine your plant after one year and decide who has the capability to become the future king."

Everyone took the seed and planted it in his pot. One of the youngsters, Joseph, took the seed home and kept it in the pot. The seed did not seem to grow into a plant in spite of his best attention. He went to his grandmother and explained the situation. She advised Joseph, "If the seed is good, it will surely grow into a plant. Allow it to remain as it is."

After one year, all youngsters **assembled** in the Central Hall of the palace. Each one of them had a well-nurtured green plant in his pot. Joseph also came there with his pot full of mud and the seed which had not grown into a plant. All others looked at Joseph's pot and started laughing. They passed comments on him. He couldn't even grow a simple plant; how could he be the king? Joseph was deeply hurt and felt ashamed of himself.

The king arrived there and looked at all the plants. He appreciated a few of them. Finally, he said, "I would like to request the young man who is standing in the last row with an empty pot to come in the front." Hearing such an announcement everyone in the Central Hall was utterly surprised.

The king further spoke, "I have found the rare display of honesty in this young man, Joseph. When I gave each of you a seed one year ago, you took it home and planted it. You thought that it would grow into a lovely plant. What you did not know, was that the seeds were boiled. They would never have **germinated** to grow into plants. All of you have replaced the boiled seeds with fresh ones and have thus got nice, green plants. Joseph, who found the seed, had not grown any plant; he was the only person to bring it back as he had taken it. He is certainly the most honest person among all of you. I think you will all agree with me that he is the best person to become my successor!"

Know These Words

valour	-	bravery
successor	-	a person who comes after another person
nurture	-	to take care of and protect someone/something
assembled	-	gathered together in one place
germinated	-	began to grow

Questions-Answers

A. Underline the correct answer.

1. The king was known for ________________.
   a. honesty b. bravery
   c. charity d. all of the above
2. The king wanted the quality of ________________.
   a. courage b. heroism
   c. honesty d. none of the above
3. What type of seeds did the king hand over?
   a. Raw seeds b. Rotten seeds
   c. Boiled seeds d. Half-grown seeds
4. The king was impressed by ________________.
   a. Joseph b. His son
   c. His relative d. No one
5. Who became the next successor?
   a. Jacob b. King's son
   c. Joseph d. None of the above

B. Answer the following questions.

1. Write the qualities that the king was known for?
   ____
2. Why did the king not choose his successor from his sons and relatives?
   ____
3. Who did the king ask to gather in the Central Hall?
   ____
4. What did the king address the assembled youngsters?
   ____
5. What did the king give to the youngsters? What did he say?
   ____

6. What happened to Joseph's seed?

____

7. Who did the king decide to choose as his successor and why?

____

8. Find the adjective used for the 'successor'.

____

Creative Writing

C. List five occasions in your life when your honest behaviour has given you immense satisfaction and five occasions when your dishonest behaviour has made you feel guilty.

Honest behaviour	*Dishonest behaviour*
_______________	_______________
_______________	_______________
_______________	_______________
_______________	_______________
_______________	_______________
_______________	_______________
_______________	_______________
_______________	_______________
_______________	_______________

Word Power

D. Give the answer in one word.

1. The quality of being honest _______________
2. Able to be trusted as being honest, safe or reliable _______________
3. A person who obeys the law _______________
4. Dishonest and likely to do illegal things, especially in order to get money _______________.

5. To give money or present to someone so that he/she may help you by doing something dishonest or illegal ____________________.

6. Extra money that you are paid in addition to your usual salary ______________.

7. A dishonest plan, especially for getting money ______________.

Grammar Skills

Past Perfect Tense

The past perfect tense is used for talking about actions that were completed before some point in the past. The formula for the past perfect these is :

had + past participle (III form of verb)

For example : 1. She **had met** him before the party.

2. I **had written** the email before he apologised.

E. Fill in the blanks using past perfect tense.

1. Kevin ___________ (go) home by the time I arrived.
2. Had they ___________ (study) English before they went to the USA?
3. Sally was embarrassed because she ___________ (forget) her dad's birthday.
4. We were hungry because we ___________ (not eat) anything since morning.
5. When I arrived at the cinema, the film ___________ (start).
6. She ___________ (live) in China before she went to Thailand.
7. He ___________ (meet) her somewhere before.
8. Julie and Anne ___________ (not/meet) before the party.
9. You ___________ (not/study) for the test, so you were very nervous.
10. I ___________ (not/take) breakfast when he arrived.

Let Us Know More

The ability to decide and choose wisely and rightly is often appreciated when problems are faced. Though we try to be as logical as possible in taking a decision, sometimes we end up making illogical choices. So, it is important to understand how people decide a particular thing to avoid a bad judgement. It would be relevant to keep in mind that a decision-making process means improving your abilities repeatedly. When you face any problem, try to know the cause of the problem and then decide the solution to the problem. Sometimes, you make a mistake in choosing the right alternative and commit a mistake in decision-making. But don't be afraid of wrong decisions, since we can learn from our past mistakes. It would be relevant to mention here that the wrong decision sometimes lays the foundation of our success in life.

Fun Chat

Read and understand the quote.

"Honest people don't hide their deeds."

20 Day and Night

We know that day and night are caused due to the rotation of the Earth on its own axis. It completes one rotation in 24 hours from west to east. In earlier days, for the people, a day meant the span of time between sunrise and sunset. We still use the word in this way to distinguish it from the period of darkness that we call night. But as **civilization** developed, it became necessary to identify daytime more accurately.

The ancient Greeks measured their day from sunrise to sunset. The Romans, unlike the Greeks, measured their day from midday to midnight. Most modern countries use Roman method.

Before mechanical clocks were invented, people had divided day and night into 12 hours each but the method proved impractical since the length of the day diers with the season. The invention of the clock helped develop a system of measuring time that is now used everywhere. Under this system, the day lasts for 24 hours from midnight to midnight. Although we no longer divide day and night into 12 hours each, we still use two periods of 12 hours each. These equal halves are distinguished by the abbreviation a.m. (ante meridiem, a Latin phrase meaning before mid-day) for the period from 12 midnight to 12 noon and p. m. (post meridiem, meaning after mid-day) for the period from 12 noon to midnight. Other ways of **splitting** up the day include the division into morning (from midnight to noon), afternoon (from noon to **dusk**), and night (from dusk to midnight). A variable period, called evening, falls between about 5 p.m. to the end of **twilight**. It is the period after sunset when the sun is only just below the **horizon**.

Know These Words

civilization	-	the stage of social and cultural development of humans
splitting	-	dividing into parts
dusk	-	the time before night when it is not yet dark; partial darkness between day and night
twilight	-	the soft glowing light from the sky when the sun is below the horizon
horizon	-	the line at which the earth's surface and the sky appear to meet

Questions-Answers

A. Underline the correct answer.

1. How many hours does the Earth take to complete its one rotation?

   a. 24 hours b. 36 hours

   c. 48 hours d. None of the above

2. The Romans measured their day from ___________.

   a. sunset to sunset b. sunrise to sunrise

   c. midnight to midnight d. sunrise to sunset

3. In which direction does the Earth rotate?

   a. North to South b. South to North

   c. East to West d. West to East

4. What is the time when the sun is below the horizon?

   a. After sunset b. Before sunset

   c. After sunrise d. Before sunrise

B. Answer the following questions.

1. How are days and night caused?

____

____

____

2. The ancient Greeks measured their day from sunset to sunset; the Romans measured it

____

____

____

3. Into how many hours and in which direction does the Earth complete its one rotation?

____

____

____

4. What do the abbreviations 'a.m.' and 'p.m.' stand for?

   a.m. – ____

   ____

   p.m. – ____

   ____

5. We cannot divide day and night into twelve hours each because

____

____

____

6. Which part of the day is usually referred to as 'evening'?

____

____

____

Creative Writing

C. Can you imagine the world without a clock or other time (-) showing devices? How would you feel when you won't be able to know the time for school, playing and T.V. shows?

____

____

____

____

____

Word Power

D. Find the words (given in the Word Bank on the next page) in the word grid.

x	f	h	e	t	i	l	t	s	e	e	f
d	s	t	q	u	l	z	w	p	r	r	k
i	u	b	u	o	b	m	i	e	e	e	i
r	m	m	a	r	m	j	n	z	h	v	n
e	m	h	t	b	p	p	t	e	p	o	d
c	e	s	o	i	s	h	e	l	s	l	i
t	r	s	r	t	n	n	r	i	c	u	r
c	q	e	m	o	o	n	b	r	g	t	e
a	e	e	z	w	n	h	f	t	e	i	c
x	h	r	o	t	a	t	i	o	n	o	t
i	h	t	r	a	e	t	v	d	e	n	e
s	y	e	a	r	t	h	w	i	a	r	a

Word Bank	axis	indirect	sphere	direct	moon
	summer	earth	orbit	tilt	equator
	evolution	winter	rotation		

Grammar Skills

Future Continuous Tense

The future continuous tense refers to an unfinished action or event that will be in progress at a time later than now. The future continuous is used for quite a few different purposes. It follows a formula of :

will + be + I form of verb + ing.

For example :

1. Robin **will be going** to the library.
2. I **shall be watching** a movie tonight.

Future Perfect Tense

The future perfect is used for indicating a future event that has a definite end-date. It follows a formula of

will + have + III form of verb (past participle)

For example :

1. The storm **will have subsided** by the time we arrive.
2. Mom **will have cooked** our favourite meal.

E. Fill in the blank using future continuous or future perfect.

1. When we arrive in Los Angeles, we'll need to rest because we ____________ about 800 miles. (drive)
2. When you get oF the train, we ______________ for you on the platform.(wait)
3. We ___________ the first train next Monday. (catch)
4. When I travel to Australia next year I ___________ English for over four years. So I think I'll be ready. (study)
5. Hurry up! The film ___________ (start) soon.
6. I am only halfway through my homework. I _______________ (not finish) it before the teacher arrives.

7. Do you think that Kate ____________ (fix) the car by evening?

8. You ____________ (retire) by the time you are 60.

Let Us Know More

The sun rises from behind the earth in the east and sinks below the earth in the west. The time when it appears is called sunrise, and the time when it disappears is called sunset. The length of time between sunrise and sunset is called daytime. In Britain, we don't have days when it is always dark, but days are longer during the time of the year when the North Pole is pointing towards the sun and shorter when it is pointing away from the sun.

Fun Chat

Riddle Time

Read and answer the riddles.

1. They come out at night without being called and are lost in the day without being stolen. What are they?
2. I pass before the sun, yet make no shadow. What am I?

21 Success is Counted Sweetest

Success is counted sweetest
By those who **ne'er** succeed.
To **comprehend** a nectar
Requires **sorest** need.
Not one of all the purple Host
Who took the Flag today
Can tell the definition
So clear of **victory**
As he **defeated** dying
On whose forbidden ear
The distant **strains** of triumph
Burst **agonized** and clear !

— Emily Dickinson

Know These Words

ne'er	–	contraction of 'never'
comprehend	–	to understand
sorest	–	painful
victory	–	success
defeated	–	having been beaten in a battle
strains	–	faint notes
agonized	–	caused mental pain

Questions-Answers

A. Fill in the blanks using the given words.

pain	*win*	*taste*	*comprehend*	*colours*
success	*need*	*defeat*	*soldiers*	*highest*

1. Those who never succeed place the ________________ value of success.
2. The poet talks about (a) ________________ who have won the war but still do not understand the real meaning of (b) ________________ because they have not experienced the (c) ________________ of failure.
3. (a) ________________, success and (b) ________________ are the major themes of the poem.
4. The word 'sorest' means ________________.
5. The people who always (a) ________________ and (b) ________________ success more often do not (c) ________________ the true (d) ________________ of success.

B. Answer the following questions.

1. What do you understand by the lines:
   Success is counted sweetest
   By those who ne'er succeed.

   ____

2. Who can understand the sweetness of nectar?

   ____

3. How do some people define success?

   ____

4. Why has the poetess used the word 'today' ?

   ____

5. What does the purple colour denote and why ?

   ____

6. Who can understand the victory more precisely—who triumphs or who gets defeated?

   ____

7. What is forbidden to the ears of the defeated soldier?

8. Find the word which means 'painful' in the poem.

9. Find out five nouns from the poem.

10. What is the rhyming scheme of the poem ?

Creative Writing

C. How would you define success?

D. How earnestly do you desire success when you perform any task?

Word Power

E. Write one word for each group of words.

1. misrepresentation of truth – ☐☐☐☐☐☐☐☐☐☐☐
2. a very large spoon – ☐☐☐☐☐
3. becoming a dad – ☐☐☐☐☐☐☐☐☐

4. people who lack success – ☐☐☐☐☐☐☐☐

5. a trip – ☐☐☐☐☐☐☐

6. restaurant enthusiast – ☐☐☐☐☐☐

7. person from Mongolia – ☐☐☐☐☐☐☐☐☐

Grammar Skills

Active Voice and Passive Voice

Active voice means that a sentence has a subject that acts upon its verb. Passive voice means that a subject is the recipient of the action of a verb.

For example :

1.	**Active**	:	The hunter killed the lion.
	Passive	:	The lion was killed by the hunter.
2.	**Active**	:	Someone has cleaned the window.
	Passive	:	The window has been cleaned.

Rules to change active voice into passive voice:

- When a verb is changed from active to passive, the object of the active verb becomes the subject of the passive verb.
- Nominative case of the pronoun is changed into objective case.
- Change the verb into III form and put a proper form 'to be' (is, am, are, was, were, be, been, being) before it according to the tense of the main verb in passive voice and the number (singular/plural) of the new subject.
- 'By' is used with the agent of action (=doer of the action). But it has to be kept in mind that where action is very important and the agent is unimportant, the preposition 'by' and the agent are left out.
- Only transitive verbs have passive voice. If an intransitive verb becomes transitive, it too can have its passive voice.
- Only eight tenses can be changed into passive voice.
- Future continuous tense and the perfect continuous tenses have no passive forms.

F. Change active voice into passive voice and vice versa.

1. The boy beat the dog.

2. Stephen kicked the soccer ball.

3. My house was robbed last night.

4. My mother is making dinner.

5. The speech was written by the President.

6. They had won the game.

7. Someone has stolen my pen.

8. Children like chocolates.

9. The government will pardon him.

Let Us Know More

All men and women want success, but only a few have it. They know the secret of success. Success comes by hard work and perseverance. A lazy man or woman cannot succeed .

A lazy student can rarely achieve good grades. If you are not prepared to work hard, you cannot expect good results.

Fun Chat

Read the quote and understand.

"People rarely succeed unless they have fun in what they are doing."

22 The Poor Man's Wealth

Jackson and Thomas were neighbours. Jackson was a poor farmer, whereas Thomas was a **landlord**.

Jackson used to stay very **relaxed** and happy. He never **bothered** to close the doors and windows of his house at night. He had a sound sleep. **Although** he had no money, his life was **peaceful**.

Thomas used to stay tense. He was very keen to close the doors and windows of his house at night. He could not sleep well. He always bothered that someone might break into his house and open his safe and steal away his money. He envied the peaceful Jackson.

One day, Thomas called Jackson and gave him a box full of cash saying,

"Look, my dear friend. I am blessed with **plenty** of wealth. Since I find you in poverty, please take this cash and live in **prosperity**."

Jackson was **overwhelmingly** happy. He was joyful throughout the day. Jackson went to bed at night as usual. But that night, he could not sleep at all. He went and closed the doors and windows. He still could not sleep. He began to keep on looking at the box of cash. The whole night he remained disturbed.

As soon as the day broke, Jackson took the box of cash to Thomas. He gave away the box to Thomas saying, "Dear Friend, I am poor. But, your money took away my peace. Please bear with me and take back your money."

Know These Words

landlord	–	a man who rents out land or a building
relaxed	–	free from tension and anxiety
bothered	–	concerned about something
although	–	in spite of the fact that; even though
peaceful	–	not involving war or violence
plenty	–	a large or sufficient amount or quantity
prosperity	–	the state of being prosperous
overwhelmingly	–	very great in amount

Questions-Answers

A. Fill in the blanks.

1. Jackson never ________ to close the doors and windows.
2. Thomas used to stay ________.
3. Thomas was blessed with plenty of ________.
4. Thomas ________ the peaceful Jackson.
5. The whole night Jackson remained ________.

B. Answer the following questions.

1. Who were neighbours and how were both of them?

____

____

2. Why did Jackson stay relaxed and happy?

____

____

3. Why did Thomas stay very tense always?

4. What did Thomas give Jackson one day and what the farmer said?

5. Was Jackson happy throughout the day?

6. How did Jackson spend his night?

7. What did Jackson do with the box at last?

Creative Writing

C. What is the value of money in our life? Is it a source of joy or unhappiness?

D. How do you spend your pocket money?

Word Power

E. Write the answer in one word.

1. a record of money a person deposits into a bank ____________
2. an Automatic machin to withdraw money ___________
3. a building in which commercial banking is transacted __________
4. the difference between credits and debits in an account _________
5. to ask for the temporary use of money on the condition of repayment and at a set rate of interest _____________
6. local office or bureau of a bank _______________
7. written order to a bank to pay the stated sum from one's account is called ___________

Grammar Skills

Direct and Indirect Speech

Direct speech repeats or quotes the exact words spoken. When we use direct speech in writing, we place the words spoken between quotation marks (" ") and there is no change in these words.

For example : 1. He said, "I live in the City Centre."
2. They said, "We have finished our work."
3. John said, "Shall we start?"

Indirect speech reports the other's words without directly quoting them. We normally change the tense of the words spoken.

For example : 1. He said that he lived in the City Centre.
2. They said that they had finished their work.
3. John asked if they should start.

In Direct Speech

1. The reported speech is put within inverted commas (" ").
2. The first word of the reported speech begins with a capital letter.

In Indirect Speech:

1. Inverted commas are not used for the reported speech which is generally introduced by the conjunction that, if, etc.
2. The comma separating the reporting verb from the reported speech is removed.
3. The tense of the reporting verb is never changed.

RULES FOR THE CHANGE OF TENSES

Conversion of assertive sentences into indirect speech:

If the reporting verb is in the present or future tense, the tense of the verb in the reported speech is not changed.

If the reporting verb is in the past tense, the tense of the reported speech will change as under:

- Simple present changes into simple past
- Present continuous changes into past continuous
- Present perfect changes into past perfect
- Simple past changes into past perfect
- Past perfect and past perfect continuous are not changed
- Shall and will of future tense become should/would

All present tenses change into their corresponding past forms:

- is, am become was; can becomes could
- are becomes were; may becomes might
- has, have become had; was/were become had been
- The forms of could, should, would, might, had are not changed

CHANGE OF PRONOUNS

- Pronouns of the first person change according to the person of the subject of the reporting verb
- Pronouns of the second person change according to the person of the objects of the reporting verb
- Pronouns of the third person remain unchanged

CHANGE OF WORDS DENOTING TIME AND POSITION

here becomes there; this becomes that; ago becomes before; today becomes that day; thus becomes so; now becomes then

CONVERSION OF QUESTIONS INTO INDIRECT SPEECH

1. The reporting verb is changed to asked, enquired, demanded, etc.
2. Whether or if is used if the reported speech begins with a helping verb or a modal, like do, does, did, is, am, are and can, could, should, would, etc.
3. All questions beginning with interrogative words, like how, what, etc., remain unchanged.
4. Interrogative form is changed into assertive form. The question mark is dropped.
5. Tenses, pronouns and words denoting nearness are changed according to the rules already stated.

F. Convert direct speech into indirect speech.

1. He said, "I can speak perfect Spanish."

   ____

   ____

2. He said, "I haven't seen Mary."

   ____

   ____

3. "Please help me!" said Noah.

   ____

   ____

4. The constable said to the man, "Have you stolen the wallet?"

   ____

   ____

5. He said, "I'll see you later."

   ____

   ____

6. She said, "I might come early."

7. "I never getup late," my mother said.

Let Us Know More

Whatever we have, we should be satisfied with it since whatever we achieve is because of our hard work. It is also true that we should be satisfied with what life gives us. It is easier to be satisfied with a little than to pursue more. Increased demands push for actions in the name of selfish desires. It is our duty to restrain ourselves and not to get indulged in rat race. We generally do not value what we have, but, we try to run after what we do not have. Always be grateful towards everything we get in our life. Always remember that to fulfil our desires we need to do hard work to earn that thing.

Fun Chat

Riddle Time

Guess the answer of the riddle.

A rich man needs something.

A poor man has something.

If you eat something you will die.

What is this 'something'?

23 Video Games – Their Impact on Children

The children of the modern world have become extremely **obsessed** with video games. Some of the children are even getting electric shocks in China for getting mad for these games.

Many children have become **insane** due to their craze for video games. They neither study nor play educational games. Since they have become addicted to video games, they remain involved in these games for more than twelve hours a day. These video games are making them crazy. Children are going out of control after the invention of these video games. Here are some practical suggestions through which children can regain their control of mind and eliminate the craze for video games.

Parents should lovingly convince their children about the bad impact of video games. They should teach them that excess of everything is bad for their physical and mental health. We should not become so much involved in something that we are not able to live without it. We must control our desires and not to do anything beyond certain limits, as it would ruin our careers and make our life miserable.

Parents should give an alternative game to their child to play with. For instance, they can bring him the cricket kit and tell him to play for an hour daily with his friends. An outdoor game is a good sport for the health and personality of a growing child. It will improve his health and make him smart and dynamic. The child should not **exceed** the limit in any sport either.

Another best alternative of video games is computer education. Parents can buy a computer for their child or admit him to a Computer Institute. The child would love to learn about software and hardware and think about to make a career in computer technology. Even if he doesn't make a career, then, at least, he would enhance his brain power and intelligence through educational programmes of computers.

But remember, the child should not be totally stopped from playing video games. He should be allowed to play video games once or twice a week, and that too for one or two hours, after the completion of his homework. Make sure you don't allow the child to become crazy for video games, else his/her entire life would become **worthless** and **miserable**.

Know These Words

obsessed	-	crazy
insane	-	mentally ill
exceed	-	to go out of the limit
worthless	-	having no value
miserable	-	being in a state of distress or unhappiness.

Questions-Answers

A. Fill in the blanks.

1. The children of the modern world have become extremely obsessed with __________.
2. Children neither __________ nor play __________.
3. An outdoor game is a good sport for __________ and __________ of a growing child.
4. By playing video games, a child's entire life can become __________ and __________.
5. Educational programmes of computer can enhance __________ and __________.
6. Excess playing of video games is bad for __________ and __________ health of a child.

B. Answer the following questions.

1. What is happening to children after the invention of video games?

____

____

2. What are the effects of craziness of video games on children?

____

____

3. What should parents teach to their children?

____

____

4. What alternative game is mentioned in the passage ?

____

____

5. What is the benefit of outdoor games?

____

____

6. What is another best alternative of video games?

____

____

7. What should be allowed to children?

____

____

8. What should not be allowed to a child?

____

____

Creative Writing

C. Do you love playing video games? How do you manage the schedule of your study and play?

____

____

____

____

____

D. What are the bad effects of video games?

____

____

____

____

Word Power

E. Write the names for these–

1. A device broadcasting visual images of stationary or moving objects ____________.
2. A game played against a computer ____________.
3. A manual control consisting of a vertical handle that can move freely in two directions used as an input ____________.
4. A portable television camera and video cassette recorder ____________.
5. An antique record player; the sound of the vibrating needle is amplified acoustically ________________.

Grammar Skills

Interjection

An interjection is a word that expresses a sudden feeling.

For example : Oh!, Alas!, Wow!, etc.

Alas! I hurt my fingers. **Wow**! Your dress is so pretty.

F. Choose the correct interjection to fill in each blank with it.

1. ______________ Does it hurt?

   a. Alas! b. Oh Dear! c. Hmm!

2. ____________________ That seems good.

   a. Hmmm! b. Hey! c. Ah!

3. ___________________ She's dead now.

   a. Hey! b. Ah! c. Alas!

4. ________________________ It's hot today.

   a. Eh! b. Yeah! c. Oh!

5. ____________________ John, how are you today ?

   a. Yeah! b. Hello! c. Ah!

6. __________________ You've stepped on my foot.

a. Ah! b. Ouch! c. Well!

G. Fill in the blanks with the appropriate interjections.

1. __________________ We have a party tomorrow.
2. __________________ You look great this morning.
3. __________________ That was the best performance to date.
4. __________________ I can' t believe; you broke my favourite toy.
5. __________________ I think I have lost my keys again.
6. __________________ I finally finished the painting.
7. __________________ You finally got your masters degree.
8. __________________ Sorry, I didn't see those skates there.
9. __________________ You have done a good job.
10. __________________ We won this match.

Let Us Know More

Video games have attracted children of all ages. The growing market of video games is a proof to its wide-spread popularity amongst children. Recent studies have shown that video games have positive as well negative impact on children. Most of the video games are creative and fun-laden. It is a good medium to get rid of stress. It also enhances the confidence level of children. Video games are responsible for making kids familiar with modern technology. Whereas playing aggressive games develops aggressive thoughts among children as well as elders. This is not a good sign. We do not want our children to spend more time playing video games as it affects their studies. Make sure to maintain balance between video games and studies.

Fun Chat

Riddle Time

Guess the answer and prove you intelligence.

Question 1. : What do you give a sick lemon?

Question 2. : How do bees get to school?

Question 3. : I am so simple that I can only point yet I guide men all over the world.

Answers

1. Friends and Flatterers

A. 1. a, b, c 2. a 3. b

B. 1. No. Because they do not stay with us in our hard times.
2. True friends are hard to find.
3. Many friends gather around us when our Wallet is full.
4. He will help us in need. He will become a part of our grief. He will also be sad with us and cry with us.
5. A true friend will always stand with us in our griefs and sorrows.
6. foe 7. faithful, flattering

E.

u	s	x	g	p	y	p	j	s	d	i	w	d	y	l
c	b	u	d	d	y	l	f	r	i	e	n	d	s	h
x	t	w	k	r	l	e	t	r	u	e	n	i	c	e
l	u	c	a	r	i	n	g	n	g	i	a	o	j	w
i	x	h	e	o	v	f	o	x	m	e	a	n	p	q
z	f	r	e	s	h	s	r	n	o	g	f	m	g	u
c	p	b	w	b	n	n	i	p	r	o	t	e	c	t
s	h	a	r	e	t	u	s	k	e	t	u	c	b	z
v	g	x	a	n	t	i	b	u	l	l	y	i	n	g
h	e	l	p	d	p	r	o	t	e	c	t	v	h	j
i	i	l	e	p	n	p	i	a	n	w	x	s	j	k
h	u	r	t	f	u	l	k	i	n	d	n	e	s	s
a	b	t	u	t	u	k	l	y	u	e	i	k	y	z
c	c	x	e	i	p	v	c	l	p	r	y	f	p	n
c	o	m	p	a	s	s	i	o	n	a	t	e	u	j

F. 1. unwrap 2. unused 3. disagree 4. unfold 5. disclose
6. misunderstand 7. misbehave 8. disconnect 9. untidy 10. dishonest

G. 1. happiness 2. sadly 3. freedom 4. friendship 5. neighbourhood
6. weakness 7. kindly 8. boredom 9. courtship 10. childhood

2. The Mysterious Passenger

A. 1. a 2. b 3. c 4. b 5. a

B. 1. The bus driver had a sound sleep at night. So, he woke up in a good mood.

2. Big John was having a strong physique and good height; that is why the bus driver hesitated in asking him the bus fare.

3. Big John was a man of six feet eight inches. He was well-built, like a wrestler whereas the driver and the conductor were only five feet each and had meek and thin stature.

4. The bus driver got fed up. He wanted to put an end to this whimsical practice of Big John.

5. He learnt judo, karate and other martial arts in the body-building programme.

6. Big John replied to him in a cool voice that he had a bus pass.

7. Yes, it is humorous. If the conductor had asked Big John the reason of not paying the fare very first day, they had not felt annoyance for so many days. And also, the driver would not have signed up the body-building programme to face Big John.

E.

l	o	r	r	y	h	h	h	a	r	a	c	y
b	e	e	y	e	e	a	a	u	o	c	o	r
i	e	t	a	e	l	n	t	t	c	r	m	a
p	p	h	c	a	i	d	r	o	k	r	p	i
l	t	o	h	i	c	c	i	m	e	i	a	z
a	u	u	t	r	o	a	c	i	t	v	c	e
n	g	s	c	c	p	r	y	n	n	e	t	p
e	b	e	h	r	t	r	c	i	c	r	c	p
b	o	b	o	a	e	r	l	v	r	b	a	e
o	a	o	p	f	r	c	e	a	a	o	r	l
a	t	a	p	t	p	a	a	n	n	a	r	i
t	e	t	e	g	c	r	e	a	e	t	r	n
a	e	e	r	a	c	t	a	l	l	i	m	o

F. 1. [.] assertive 2. [?] interrogative 3. [!] exclamation 4. [.] imperative
5. [?] interrogative 6. [?] interrogative 7. [!] exclamation 8. [.] imperative
9. [?] interrogative 10. [.] assertive

Brainy Riddles

1. It is a single–storey house, and hence, there is no staircase.
2. An egg
3. Because he is alive.
4. He throws the ball upwards.

3. How to Improve Your Memory

A 1. concentrate 2. exams of life 3. I can't do 4. comfortable

B. 1. Meditation is the best method to sharpen our memory within a short span of time.

2. Practise meditation daily for at least 15 minutes and we would see remarkable results in our memory power within the next 15 days.

3. Eat a nutritious diet that includes green vegetables, sprouted beans, salads and fruit for a good memory. Some dried fruits, like almonds are also very good for memory. We can take them with hot milk.

4. Revision of lessons can enhance our memory. We must try to understand our lessons first. Then we should revise them for at least five times to attempt our exam efficiently.

5. Look carefully at the things around you and then close your eyes. Try to recollect as many things as you can. This method can enhance your concentration.

6. We must sharpen our memory skills to be able to pass all the exams of life with flying colours.

E.

1 k															
n															
o		2 l			3 h	e	4 a	r	t						
5 w	r	i	t	e			c								
		f					c								
	6 b	e	7 l	i	e	v	e								
			i				p						8 g		
			a				9 t	e	10 s	t	i	m	o	n	y
11 e	t	e	r	n	a	l			o				d		
									n						

F. 1. plastic 2. iron 3. wood 4. cotton 5. flour

G. 1. flowers 2. bear 3. cookies 4. car 5. egg

4. Letter from a Parent

A. 1. The son had written too many family life details in the essay.

2. laugh when there was a break for lunch at mid-day.

3. was his parent.

4. after all, he had done his work.

5. teacher.

6. I trust you will not blame my son.

7. a. Tom writes the essay.

   b. The essay contains too many family life details.

   c. The parent feels them unfit to be read in the class.

   d. The parent tears the essay.

D. 1. hear 2. Nay 3. a. die, b. dye 4. a. hare, b. hair

E. 1-e 2-h 3-a 4-f 5-c 6-g 7-d 8-b

F. 1. wisdom 2. pride 3. kindness 4. knowledge

5. courage 6. intelligence 7. location 8. agreement

9. attachment 10. childhood 11. attraction 12. argument

5. Pride Hath A Fail

A. 1. b 2. a 3. a 4. c 5. a

B. 1. The mango tree was very tall, strong and stout. It was very proud of its stature and used to mock at the other trees and plants, especially those who were very lean and thinly built.

2. The paddy plant used to swing in happiness every day while the wind blew. He was so happy that he never felt sorrow for his thinly structure.

3. The mango tree called the paddy plant a cursed child as he didn't have even strength to bear the load of a small bee.

4. A fierce storm uprooted the proud mango tree and made the tree fell with a deep and heavy thud.

5. The paddy plant managed to save his life due to his frail and fragile physique.

6. The paddy plant thanked God for sending him in this beautiful world. He always expressed his indebtedness to God for it.

7. God blesses us by bestowing good health, comfort and success but we should not be proud of it. Rather, we should thank Him for His blessings.

D.

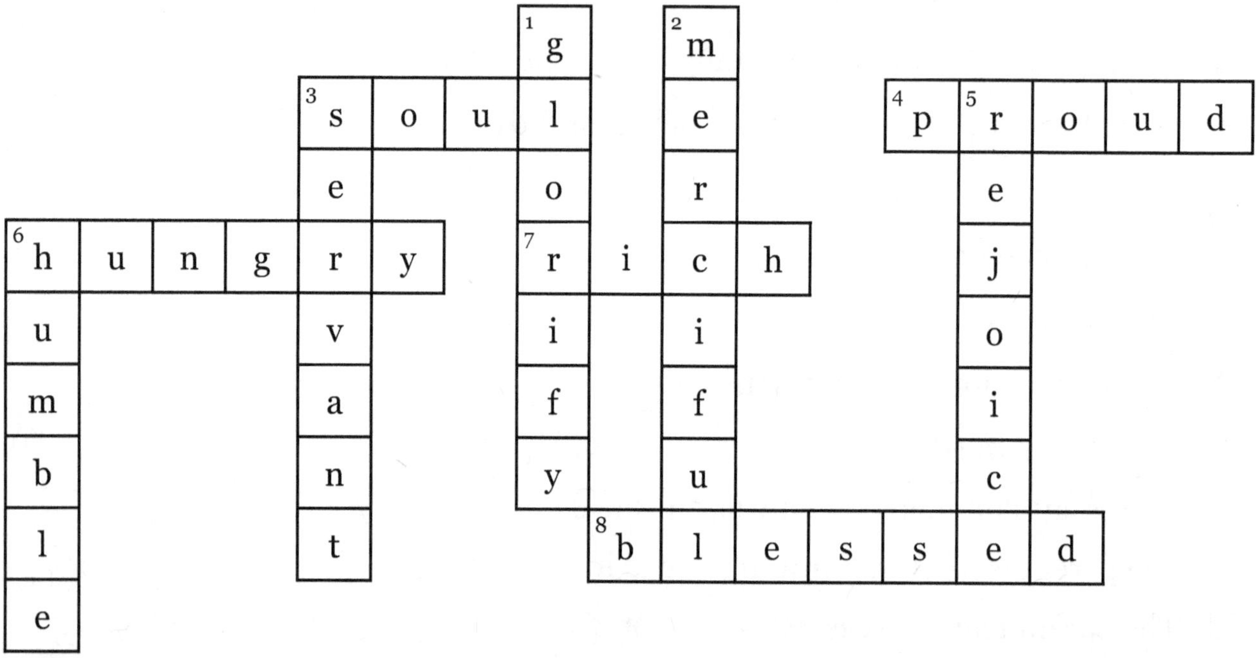

E. 1. The bus stopped for him.
2. They bought a dress.
3. They fought against them.
4. The teacher loved them.
5. Count these
6. The boys are tall. They can reach the top of the shelf.

F. 2. This room is his.
3. That house is theirs.
4. These books are theirs.
5. Those balls were ours.
6. This pen was hers.
7. Those trees are yours.
8. This kitchen is ours

6. Importance of Prayer

A. 1. a   2. c   3. a   4. c

B. 1. The people of the modern world have forgotten God and are wasting their time and money on useless pursuits.
2. God has formed numerous plants, animals, men, demigods, suns, moons, stars and planets with His energy.
3. God is the destroyer of devils. He gives rewards to the righteous and punishes sinners. So, one should pray to God daily.
4. Modernity means to become cultured, decent, sophisticated and fashionable, but it doesn't mean to forget God.
5. We must understand that all beggars, the handicapped and the poorest of the poor that we see, are suffering from the punishments of forgetting God.
6. The persons who forget God are the greatest sinners on the earth. They are bound to suffer from dire consequences for their evil deeds.
7. If we want success, wealth and honour in the world, then we should never forget to pray to God from our heart, soul and mind every day.

E.

										1 p		2 b			
					3 f	a	v	o	u	r		l			
	4 p				r					i		i			
5 p	r	o	6 p	h	e	t				s		7 n	e	w	s
	e		o		e			g	8	o	d				
	a		o		d					n					
	c		r		o					e					
	h				m			9 s	c	r	o	l	l		

F. 1. herself
2. themselves
3. herself
4. themselves
5. herself
6. myself
7. ourselves
8. itself

Fun Chat : 1. Popcorn.
2. He was walking, not driving. (This riddle adds irrelevant information to deceive the reader. You expect that since he's a bus driver, he's currently driving the bus — but it never actually says that!)

7. Students and Discipline

A. 1. c 2. b 3. a 4. b 5. a

B. 1. Discipline means complete obedience to certain rules and regulations.
2. A student's life is a period of learning and grooming.
3. A student needs to be sincere, dedicated, firm and focused to his goals.
4. He should learn to face difficult situations and win over them.
5. His mind will be strong and sharp only when he is physically strong, fit and healthy.
6. When discipline is enforced, it fails to bring the desired result. True essence of discipline is lost when it is enforced. The man becomes more a machine and less a human being.
7. a. He should be very regular and sincere to his studies.
b. He should be hard-working.
c. He should remain active and smart.
d. He should be healthy and fit.
e. A student should be very devoted and sincere to his studies.

8. A student's life is the formative period. The foundation of adulthood is laid down during that time. The man grows with the habits and manners acquired at that time. These things hardly change. So, a student should be much disciplined during his school days.

9. a. cooperative b. sincere c. smart

E.

cowardly timid	old ancient	huge enormous	puny small	rash reckless

F.

wild tame	often seldom	proud humble	bright dull	smile frown

G. 1. Neither 2. Either 3. Neither 4. Either 5. Neither

H. 1. Show me the way which leads to the school.

2. He is the man who never satisfies.

3. This is the woman whose son has gone to the U.S.A.

4. The beggar whom we helped was blind.

5. This is the house which belongs to my uncle.

8. Which Loved Best?

A. 1. a. He went to play on the swing in his yard.

2. b. His mother had to bring in wood to burn in the family's stove.

3. b. Her mother was relieved because she was tired of hearing her remarks and seeing her frustration.

4. a. I'm glad that there is no school today.

B. 1. The mother had four children.

2. Three of them John, Nell and Fan said that they loved the mother.

3. John could have helped his mother by bringing wood for making food.

4. She was happy as she was tired of seeing her frustration and hearing her remarks.

5. Fan helped her mom out of great love which kept her happy all day.

6. Fan loved the mother best as she tried to give her mother all the comfort that she could.

7. 1. She - be 2. said - bed 3. broom-room

E. 1. to win the first prize (noun phrase)

2. in the brown frock (noun phrase)

3. with care (adverb phrase)

4. at Victoria Terminal (adverb phrase)

5. in a loud voice (adverb phrase)

6. very delicious (adjective phrase)

7. dark and brown (adjective phrase)

F.

e	i	e	f	a	s	c	i	n	a	t	i	o	l	o	v	e
c	a	f	o	n	d	n	e	s	s	o	m	e	v	a	a	s
o	s	l	f	a	y	c	c	p	l	n	c	o	n	t	d	p
m	t	l	a	d	e	d	i	c	a	t	e	s	t	e	e	e
a	t	t	a	c	h	m	e	n	t	d	o	r	n	l	v	e
l	e	r	r	s	l	g	h	g	o	m	a	i	i	s	o	e
i	m	e	n	d	e	v	o	t	e	d	n	e	s	s	t	a
n	e	m	e	m	r	l	a	n	t	e	h	n	e	u	e	a
e	n	e	n	d	e	a	r	m	e	n	t	l	t	z	d	r
s	i	n	s	n	l	s	o	o	p	t	i	i	a	r	n	y
s	d	e	v	o	t	i	o	n	i	c	r	w	r	j	e	r
f	e	r	n	s	l	c	l	s	a	h	s	c	t	r	s	t
e	r	e	l	s	n	i	i	c	c	t	l	r	i	o	s	e
s	s	o	p	a	s	s	i	o	n	a	t	e	s	m	o	m
s	y	i	c	e	q	u	u	l	s	o	f	r	t	a	k	m

9. An Invaluable Gift of Love

A. 1. a 2. c 3. d 4. b 5. c

B. 1. She took a piece of golden wrapping paper from her father's collection.

2. He asked his daughter, "What are you doing with this paper? Don't you know how costly this paper is? I have bought this paper to use for my own purpose, and you are wasting it."
3. The little daughter pouted her lips. Tears rolled down from her eyes, unnoticed by her father.
4. The next morning the girl came to her father with a gift wrapped with the golden paper.
5. When he unwrapped the box and opened it, he found nothing inside it. Again, he was very angry.
6. After a few months, the little girl met with an accident and died.
7. Suddenly, he discovered the gift-box given by his little daughter.
8. He kept that box by his bedside for many years, and, whenever he felt discouraged, he would take out an imaginary kiss and remember the love of his daughter who had put it in there.

D.

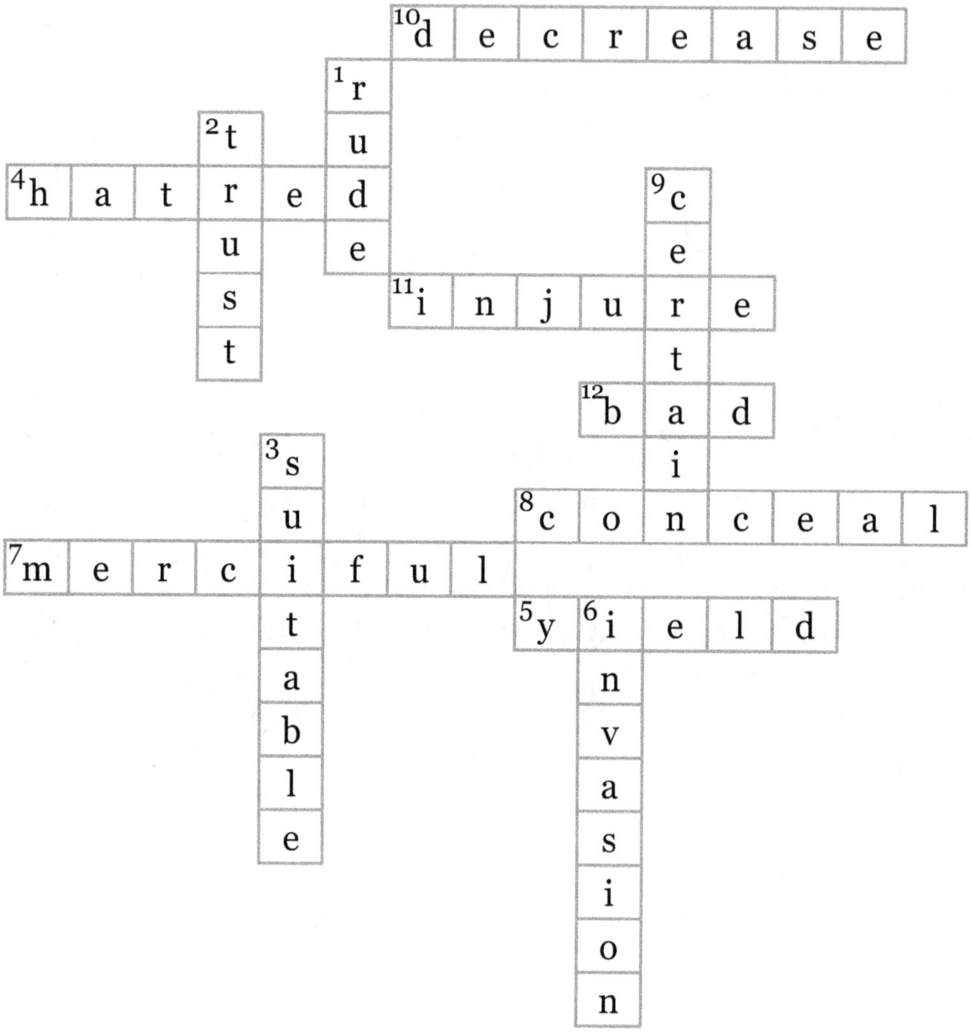

E. 1. especially when her father asked her to take part.
2. When he was standing next to his sister.
3. which seemed never-ending.
4. Even though he had little patience.
5. although she had not been playing for long.

10. Etiquette and Good Manners

A. 1. Good manners
2. action, speech
3. social, cultural
4. pleasantly
5. behaviour
6. culture, good education

B. 1. Good manners reveal a person's upbringing.
2. A cultured and educated person is always well-mannered. His behaviour with others is always pleasant.
3. The way you reflect your manners, others also do the same. Good manners also reflect good conduct and character.
4. We judge a tree by its leaves and fruit and people judge a person by his/her behaviour.

5. Childhood is the best age to learn good manners. A child can quickly and easily learn things and adapt itself.
6. It requires a strong will, discipline, self-control and desire to learn good manners.

E.

o	p	a	r	d	e	w	f	a	i	r	n	e	s	s
b	e	t	s	a	j	t	i	l	p	e	o	f	m	l
f	r	i	e	n	d	s	h	i	p	s	o	r	w	t
m	s	a	l	c	a	t	r	e	s	p	e	c	t	u
r	e	b	f	c	e	w	r	t	s	o	o	w	n	i
q	v	m	d	c	i	t	i	z	e	n	s	h	i	p
l	e	k	i	u	t	l	v	e	a	s	l	a	e	t
t	r	u	s	t	w	o	r	t	h	i	n	e	s	s
e	a	w	c	r	y	b	e	m	n	b	l	o	e	r
b	n	y	i	v	g	r	l	k	e	i	h	a	d	j
u	c	j	p	a	b	x	e	b	g	l	o	v	w	a
y	e	o	l	b	h	i	c	a	r	i	n	g	p	h
m	g	n	i	l	g	m	e	a	h	t	r	t	l	o
w	h	e	n	h	o	n	e	s	t	y	g	o	u	i
a	u	w	e	q	j	u	c	o	u	r	a	g	e	t

F. 1. who 2. which 3. who 4. who 5. that 6. which 7. who

G. 1. The old man and woman who wrote this book, lived in this house before we did.
2. The student who cheated was banned from taking the exam.
3. The young man who wants to meet my father, has just arrived.
4. The famous library which was inaugurated by our Principal, is situated in this city.
5. The spaceship which landed on Mars, is on display here.

11. Childhood

A. 1. there is no real existence of heaven and hell as it could not be geographically located on any map.
2. were not all they pretended to be, talked and preached love, but did not act so lovingly.
3. he can choose on his own way, guided by his mind now capable of producing thoughts and opinions that are different from those of other people.
4. he knows that it has gone to some forgotten place or hidden in an infant's face.

B.

Child	Adult
carefree	complex and frustrated
always cool, happy	show off, copying

less worried	full of worries
Free to do anything	full of anxieties
Less restricted	having fear of profit and loss

C. At the age of twelve, the poet realised that hell and heaven were not real but mere stories and science didn't support the existence of hell and heaven as they cannot be found on any map.

D. The poet believes that he has lost his childhood. He believes so because he has lost the innocence and purity of his childhood. When he was a child, he used to believe in the existence of hell and heaven. He also believed that adults had real love. In his childhood, he didn't have any egoistic attitude.

E. The poet finds his lost childhood on the face of a child. He can get it back only when he commits to be a child again, forgetting the complex adult concepts and perceptions.

G. Friendship

friend	ship	sin	
pine	end	fried	
hip	dish	red	
drip	hide	hid	pen
fins	ride	pin	

Happiness

pin	snap
happen	shape
snip	app
sin	his
paise	shapes
nip	par
pen	

H. 1. quickly
2. excitedly
3. carelessly
4. slowly
5. finally
6. easily
7. suddenly
8. beautifully

12. The Farmer and the Snake

A. 1. c 2. d 3. a 4. c 5. a 6. c

B. 1. The farmer used to go to his farmyard every morning for harvesting crops.
2. They found a snake lying on the road. It was unnable to move due to cold.
3. The farmer and his son felt pity for it. The farmer took the snake in his lap. Instead of going to the farmyard, they came back to their residence.
4. The farmer took the snake near a fire-place and kept near it for some minutes. It made the snake fresh and move inside the room.

5. He asked the farmer's son, "Come; let us play together." The farmer's son replied, "No, I don't have enough time to play. I am going to the farmyard with my father."
6. It was very angry with the farmer's son, hence it tried to bite him.
7. The farmer killed the snake with a stick.

E.

b	a	p	a	b	h	s	p	i	t	m	t	l	e	a	a	d	o
e	d	o	d	e	y	t	r	z	q	o	y	e	a	e	t	a	d
e	r	n	e	e	r	a	t	e	u	s	u	a	r	o	s	m	r
t	r	d	f	p	x	g	s	d	g	q	i	f	w	p	f	s	d
l	d	s	g	d	i	b	q	s	y	u	o	h	i	a	j	e	s
e	o	k	t	s	y	e	i	d	p	i	p	o	g	p	f	l	x
a	a	a	u	s	p	e	o	u	s	t	a	p	z	e	d	f	z
s	n	t	i	y	i	t	p	t	y	o	e	p	e	r	t	l	o
t	t	e	o	u	o	l	u	d	m	a	t	e	o	w	z	y	p
x	p	r	p	i	l	e	x	s	o	t	u	r	d	a	h	d	z
y	i	o	s	d	a	e	t	i	t	i	z	r	l	s	i	a	d
a	m	b	u	s	h	b	u	g	h	k	o	o	f	p	l	e	k
c	o	c	k	r	o	a	c	h	z	u	o	p	u	o	x	p	l
t	l	a	c	e	w	i	n	g	a	s	e	t	i	o	v	u	e
b	e	d	b	u	g	v	s	t	i	n	k	b	u	g	y	e	a
t	a	u	i	p	o	y	h	o	v	e	r	f	l	y	u	d	f
v	c	r	i	c	k	e	t	d	f	a	d	h	g	a	c	d	e
a	p	h	i	d	f	h	a	h	j	o	p	d	a	e	y	u	j

F.

1.	yesterday	(Adverb of time)	6. patiently	(Adverb of manner)
2.	lazily	(Adverb of manner)	7. there	(Adverb of place)
3.	loudly	(Adverb of manner)	8. merrily	(Adverb of manner)
4.	often	(Adverb of frequency)	9. gracefully	(Adverb of manner)
5.	extremely	(Adverb of degree)	10. everywhere	(Adverb of place)

13. Tale of Three Fishes

A. 1. a 2. c 3. b 4. d

B. 1. They discussed, "This pond is full of fish, and there are many big ones too. We have never caught fish in this pond. Let us come back tomorrow morning to catch the fish."

2. He immediately assembled all other fish and told them what they had heard. He said, "Tomorrow morning the fishermen will arrive to catch us. I do not want to die like this. So, I will leave with my family at the earliest. I advise all of you to follow me. It will not be wise for anybody to stay here any longer."

3. He mocked at the other two fishes, and said "See how cowardly these two act ! This pond belongs to our forefathers,and it is our home. For so long, no harm has ever been done to the fish of this pond."
4. He further said, "O friends, the scriptures state that when the time for one's death arrives, no one is spared. If death has to come, let us rather die bravely in our home!"
5. By evening, the families of the first two fishes started their journey to a different pond through a small outlet. They were followed by many fish who believed in them.
6. The next morning the fishermen arrived as per their plan and trapped all the fish that remained in the pond by casting their nets all over the pond.
7. The fishermen were overjoyed with the big haul of fish that they had caught.

D.

	1 f	o	l	l	o	w
	i					
	s			2 j		3 b
4 s	h	o	r	e		o
i				5 s	e	a
6 n	e	t		u		t
k				s		

E. 1.beautiful
2. red
3. rich
4. better
5. useful
6. good
7. glorious
8. small, great
9. curly
10. harsh

14. Importance of Books

A. 1. Education Master.
2. eliminate many misunderstandings caused between friends or relatives, improves the relations among them.
3. entertainment.
4. imagination, strengthens the use of language, simplifies difficult tasks.
5. all the queries of mind, satiate our thirst of knowledge.
6. soulful bedtime stories.

B. 1. They impart valuable knowledge and instructions to mankind and make the citizens of a country worthy.
2. The entire mankind can uplift its body, mind and soul through knowledge gained from good books.
3. Some of the autobiographies of great personalities give us great lessons and we learn to correct our own mistakes after knowing the consequences of our wrong deeds from the experiences of great leaders.
4. We can read and enjoy them in our journey. We can go through good books in our bedrooms, drawing rooms or whenever we have some spare time.

5. Literature is valuable for many reasons as it enhances children's creativity and imagination; introduces them to new people, places and ideas; builds their vocabulary and strengthens their use of language; and simplifies difficult tasks with simple solutions.
6. Books enhance the love between parents and children. Some children love to snuggle up to their parents for soulful bedtime stories.
7. We should expose our children to quality books of all kinds, be it picture, story, rhymes and rhyming, adventure and mystery, fantasy, interpersonal relationships, travel, reference, riddles and puzzles, art and science. This way reading will become a treasured part of our children's life.

E.

b	d	x	r	t	s	b	n	m	w	u	i	r	a	t	c	t	t
e	b	o	y	d	u	m	p	l	i	n	g	g	n	o	l	h	o
a	f	r	t	g	s	r	t	t	n	i	r	f	g	i	a	e	b
u	d	s	h	a	p	i	g	h	n	s	e	b	e	l	r	w	e
t	d	a	e	d	e	f	g	e	i	d	e	a	l	u	a	o	a
y	d	v	l	e	t	i	o	i	e	l	n	k	i	y	c	r	k
a	x	l	i	o	n	f	i	s	t	p	e	e	n	l	t	l	i
n	t	c	t	b	b	n	w	l	h	l	g	t	b	u	h	d	d
d	y	r	t	b	o	t	f	a	e	h	g	l	e	y	e	o	b
t	d	t	l	f	t	d	j	n	p	r	s	s	i	t	s	l	n
h	t	b	e	t	f	i	s	d	o	b	a	t	j	c	n	c	m
e	d	t	p	u	d	g	u	o	o	p	n	a	i	y	o	i	l
b	t	f	r	v	d	s	y	f	h	d	d	r	n	h	w	t	b
e	a	m	i	i	r	e	s	q	u	i	h	b	g	p	y	i	t
a	s	f	n	o	g	f	i	s	h	o	a	t	y	c	d	e	t
s	l	o	c	f	i	s	h	d	t	g	m	z	u	d	a	s	s
t	b	a	e	k	e	t	s	t	a	r	t	y	d	r	y	t	t
t	h	e	s	e	c	r	e	t	k	i	n	g	d	o	m	t	o

F. 1. best
2. busiest
3. mightier
4. handsome
5. shallow
6. high
7. difficult, most difficult

Riddle Time :

1. 6 painters
2. Library

15. The Fallen Leaves

A. a. first leaf
b. siblings
c. clung
d. fallen
e. fire of spring
f. withered
g. sleep softly
h. winter
i. soil
j. decay
k. leaves
l. May

B. 1. all the leaves of that branch have fallen.
2. when the leaves decay, they change into a fine compost, which helps in the good growth of the plants in the spring season.

E. 1. of 2. in 3. about 4. of 5. of, for
6. on behalf of 7. with 8. for/at 9. down 10. at
11. by 12. with 13. up 14. in 15. towards

F. 1. Joseph is slow at English. 2. I am tired of false excuses.
3. Let's hope for the best. 4. I did it for your good.
5. The milk is in the glass.

G.

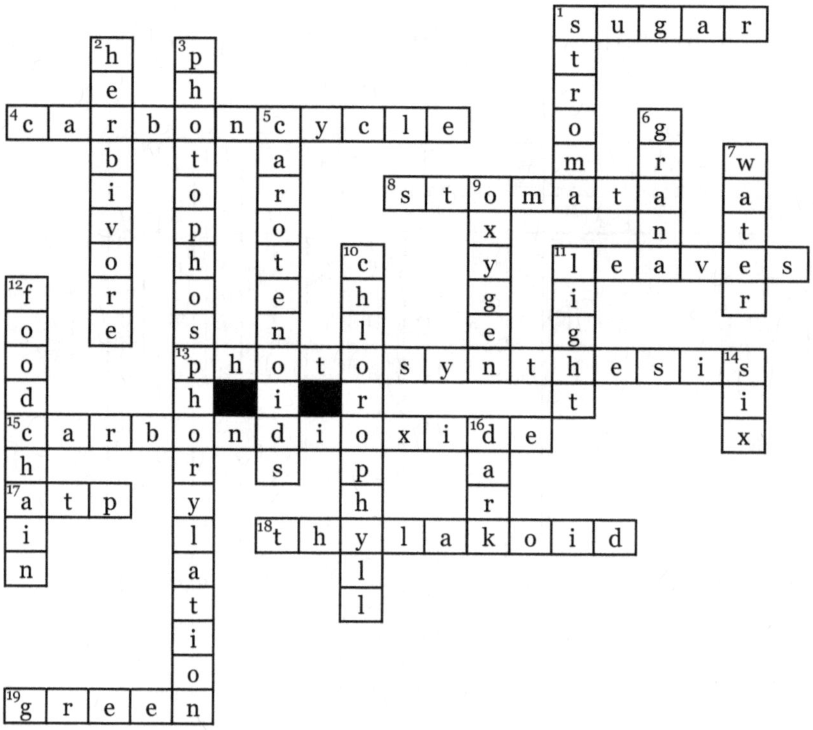

16. The Cobra and the Crows

A. 1. b 2. c 3. c 4. a 5. b 6. c

B. 1. Two crows-husband and wife-lived on the banyan tree. A cobra also lived in the hollow of the same tree.
2. The crows had a problem because the black cobra would climb up the tree and eat the newborns, whenever the female crow hatched her eggs.
3. The crows went to a jackal, who lived in a nearby banyan tree, to seek his advice.
4. The jackal replied, "Please don't give up. Even a powerful enemy can be overcome with the use of wit."
5. The female crow noticed wealthy women swimming in a lake. They had left gold and pearl necklaces on the banks of the lake, which were being guarded by the royal servants.
6. At once, the female crow swooped down and picked up a big necklace in her beak, and started flying slowly.
7. She dropped the necklace in front of the hollow of the tree, where the black cobra was asleep.

8. The servants attacked the cobra with sticks and stones to recover the necklace. They killed the wicked cobra.

E.

r	g	l	i	z	a	r	d	g	o	a	t	u	a
c	l	f	h	e	l	t	r	u	t	e	s	r	i
a	u	s	g	h	s	n	a	k	e	u	h	a	g
t	i	n	u	a	i	e	r	b	i	r	d	l	u
t	a	a	i	m	i	f	l	g	b	d	o	i	a
u	g	k	n	s	a	f	t	e	s	s	l	b	n
s	t	e	e	t	b	o	t	u	r	t	l	e	a
d	e	f	a	e	e	m	t	l	r	f	e	e	g
i	r	b	p	r	g	o	i	g	a	o	l	g	a
t	g	h	i	h	r	u	u	h	t	t	a	i	e
d	k	u	g	r	i	s	c	h	i	c	k	e	n
o	a	b	a	a	r	e	d	f	e	r	r	e	t
g	t	n	r	n	a	u	d	u	a	a	t	s	k
f	i	s	h	i	c	h	o	p	p	e	r	o	h

F. 1. is pushing 2. is flattering 3. am taking 4. are catching
5. are playing 6. is playing 7. am ironing 8. is taking

17. Public Relations

A. 1. c 2. d 3. a 4. c 5. b

B. 1. A man who doesn't know how to keep cordial relations with people around him, can never attain success in his life.

2. We should be down-to-earth and remain away from artificialities, false pretensions of life, to please people.

3. After gaining knowledge about the people around us, talk or chat about their likes and dislikes. Listen to them more and talk less. Talk politely in a low tone so that they may not get irriated.

4. Never insult or degrade anyone around you. If you want to correct their faults, then you should mention his qualities along with his flaws.

5. Only condemning and degrading others in the public is not good.

6. We must realise that we too are human beings who can commit mistakes, like others and, thus, nobody is perfect on this earth.

7. Even great leaders, writers, sportsmen and film stars are also not perfect. They may be

better than others in understanding or sensibility but they may also commit mistakes in their life.

8. We ought to correct our own flaws first, before correcting others. This is the best way to imporve our relationship with the people around us and to achieve success in life.

E. 1. Press agent 2. public opinion 3. two-way communication
4. dialogue 5. clarity 6. goal

F. 1. I have not worked 2. have bought 3. have not planned
4. has spoken 5. has not got

G. 1. I've studied French.
2. She has eaten an octopus.
3. We have read that book.
4. He has lived here for three years.
5. They have missed the train.
6. She has gone to Peru.
7. You have found your wallet.
8. She has passed the exam.

18. Breakfast

A. 1. a. walk b. delight c. old man
d. eggs and bacon e. best meal f. prefer lunch or dinner.

B. a. perfectly laid out b. I was extremely hungry
c. passage of time d. respect and offer with happiness

D.

D.

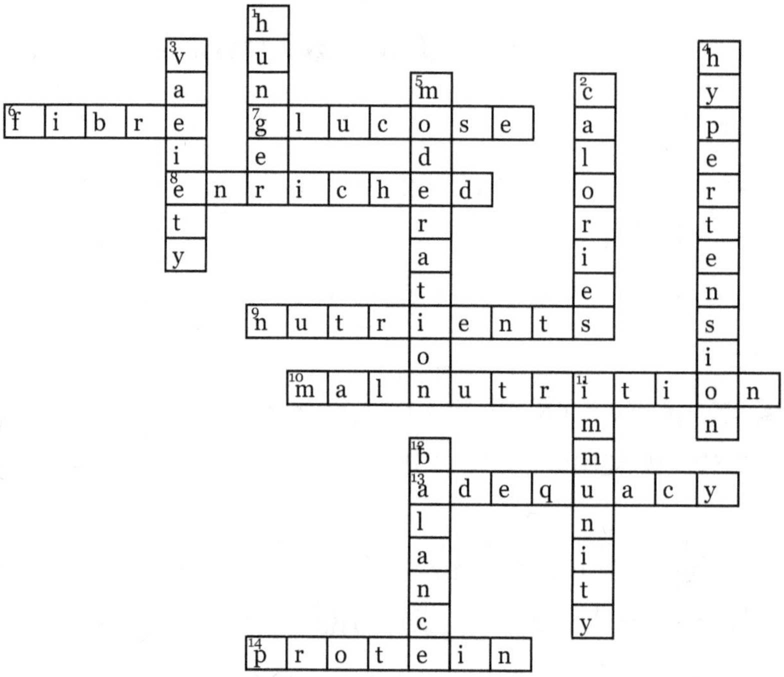

E. 1. was sleeping 2. was reading 3. were eating
4. was using 5. were cooking 6. were not playing
7. was not listening

Riddle Time:

1. Frosted flakes
2. Dinner

19. Honesty

A. 1. d. 2. c 3. c 4. a 5. c

B. 1. The king was known for his truthfulness, charity and valour.
2. He could not choose his sons and relatives as his successor because he thought that they were not honest.
3. He asked the youth of his kingdom to gather in the Central Hall of the palace.
4. He addressed them, "My dear children, I want to choose the next king of this country so that the people of this country may remain safe."
5. He handed over a seed to everyone. He asked them to keep the seed in a pot, nurture it and grow it. He further said that he would examine their plants after one year and decide who had the capability to become the future king.
6. Joseph's seed did not grow into a plant in spite of his best efforts.
7. The king decided to choose Joseph as his successor since he was certainly the most honest person among all of them.
8. honest

D. 1. honesty 2. trustworthy 3. law observer 4. crooked
5. bribe 6. bonus 7. scam

E. 1. had gone 2. studied 3. had forgetten 4. had not eaten
5. had started 6. had lived 7. had met 8. hadn't met
9. had not studied 10. hadn't taken

20. Day and Night

A. 1. a. 2. c 3. d 4. a

B. 1. Days and nights are caused due to the rotation of the Earth on its axis.
2. from midnight to midnight.
3. The Earth completes its one rotation in 24 hours from west to east.
4. ante meridiem. (before midday)
post meridiem. (after midday)
5. Length of the day differs with the seasons.
6. The part of the day between about 5 p.m. and end of the twilight.

D.

x	f	h	e	t	i	l	t	s	e	e	f
d	s	t	q	u	l	z	w	p	r	r	k
i	u	b	u	o	b	m	i	e	e	e	i
r	m	m	a	r	m	j	n	z	h	v	n
e	m	h	t	b	p	p	t	e	p	o	d
c	e	s	o	i	s	h	e	l	s	l	i
t	r	s	r	t	n	n	r	i	c	u	r
c	q	e	m	o	o	n	b	r	g	t	e
a	e	e	z	w	n	h	f	t	e	i	c
x	h	r	o	t	a	t	i	o	n	o	t
i	h	t	r	a	e	t	v	d	e	n	e
s	y	e	a	r	t	h	w	i	a	r	a

E. 1. shall have driven 2. shall be waiting 2. shall be catching 4. shall have studied
5. shall be starting 6. shall not have finished 7. shall have fixed 8. shall have retired

Riddle Time:

1. Stars 2. The wind

21. Success is Counted Sweetest

A. 1. a. highest 2. soldiers b. success c. pain
3. a. Need b. defeat
4. painful
5. a. win b. taste c. comprehend d. colours

B. 1. These lines state that those who have never succeeded, really crave success the most.
2. The one who is thirsty can understand the sweetness of nectar.
3. Some people define success by virtue of positions that they acquire and assume in life.
4. The poetess has used the word 'today' to define the presentness and transiency of the situation.
5. The purple colour denotes the royalty since the fine clothes/robes of kings and emperors were dyed purple.
6. According to the poetess, the one who loses the battle and is dying can perceive success better.
7. Sound of success is forbidden to his ears.

8. Sorest

9. a. success b. nectar c. host d. flag e. victory

10. The rhyming scheme of the poem is ABCB.

E. 1. distortions 2. ladle 3. fathering 4. failures
5. stumble 6. foodie 7. Mongolian

F. 1. The dog was beates by the boy.
2. The soccer ball was kicked by Stephen.
3. Someone robbed my house last night.
4. Dinner was being made by my mother.
5. The President wrote the speech.
6. The game had been won by them.
7. My pen has been stolen.
8. Chocolates are liked by children.
9. He will be pardoned by the government.

22. The Poor Man's Wealth

A. 1. bothered 2. tense 3. wealth 4. envied 5. disturbed

B. 1. Jackson and Thomas were neighbours. Jackson was a poor farmer. He always stayed relaxed and happy. Thomas was a landlord. He always stayed tense.
2. He had no money; therefore, he was peaceful.
3. Thomas used to be very tense always. He was very keen to close the doors and windows of his house. He was always bothered that someone might break open his safe and steal away his money. Therefore, he always stayed very tense.
4. One day, Thomas gave Jackson a boxful of cash saying, "Look, my dear friend; I am blessed with plenty of wealth. Since I find you in poverty, please take this cash and live in prosperity."
5. Yes. He was joyful throughout the day.
6. Jackson went to bed at night as usual. But that night, he could not sleep at all. He went and closed the doors and windows. He still could not sleep. He began to keep looking at the box of cash. The whole night he remained disturbed.
7. Jackson took the box of cash to Thomas and gave him back saying, "Dear friend, I am poor. But, your money took away my peace. Please bear with me and take back your money."

E. 1. account 2. ATM 3. bank 4. balance
5. borrow 6. branch 7. cheque

F. 1. He said that he could speak perfect Spanish.
2. He said that he hadn't seen Mary.

3. The constable asked the man if he had stolen the wallet.
4. Mother asked James if he had done his homework.
5. He said that he would see me later.
6. She said that she might come early.
7. My mother said that she never got up late.

Riddle Time: Something is nothing because a rich man needs nothing; a poor man has nothing and if you eat nothing you'll die.

23. Video Games – Their Impact on Children

A. 1. video games 2. study, educational games
3. health, personality 4. worthless, miserable
5. brain power, intelligence 6. physical, mental

B. 1. Video games are making children crazy. Children are going out of control after the invention of video games.
2. Children neither study nor play educational games. Since they have become so much addicted to video games, they remain involved in them for more than twelve hours a day.
3. Parents should teach their children that excess of everything is bad for their mental and physical health. We should not become so much involved in anything that we are not able to live without it.
4. Cricket, an outdoor game.
5. An outdoor game is a good sport for the health and personality of a growing child. It will improve his/her health and make his/her smart and dynamic.
6. Another best alternative of video games is computer education.
7. Children should be allowed to play video games once or twice a week, and that too for one or two hours, after the completion of their homework.
8. He should not be allowed to become crazy for video games, else his entire life would become worthless and miserable.

E. 1. Oh Dear! 2. Ah! 3. Alas! 4. Eh! 5. Hello! 6. Ouch!

F. 1. Hurray! 2. Wow! 3. Bravo! 4. What! 5. Uh! 6. Yipee!
7. Congrats! 8. Oops! 9. Bravo 10. Hurray!

G. 1. Television 2. Video game 3. Joystick 4. Camcorder 5. Gramophone

Fun Chat :

1. Lemon aid 2. On the school buzz 3. Compass

www.ingramcontent.com/pod-product-compliance
Lightning Source LLC
LaVergne TN
LVHW060451061126
851857LV00016B/1787
9789391460747